TWAYNE'S WORLD

A Survey of the W

Sylvia E. Bowman, Indiana University

GENERAL EDITOR

FRANCE

Maxwell A. Smith, Guerry Professor of French, Emeritus
The University of Chattanooga
Former Visiting Professor in Modern Languages
The Florida State University

EDITOR

Michel Butor

(TWAS 275)

TWAYNE'S WORLD AUTHORS SERIES (TWAS)

The purpose of TWAS is to survey the major writers—novelists, dramatists, historians, poets, philosophers, and critics—of the nations of the world. Among the national literatures covered are those of Australia, Canada, China, Eastern Europe, France, Germany, Greece, India, Italy, Japan, Latin America, the Netherlands, New Zealand, Poland, Russia, Scandinavia, Spain, and the African nations, as well as Hebrew, Yiddish, and Latin Classical literature. This survey is complemented by Twayne's United States Authors Series and English Authors Series.

The intent of each volume in these series is to present a critical-analytical study of the works of the writer; to include biographical and historical material that may be necessary for understanding, appreciation, and critical appraisal of the writer; and to present all material in clear, concise English—but not to vitiate the scholarly content of the work by doing so.

Michel Butor

By MICHAEL SPENCER

Monash University, Victoria, Australia

Twayne Publishers, Inc.　：：　New York

ISBN 0-8057-2186-X

MANUFACTURED IN THE UNITED STATES OF AMERICA

To Mary

Preface

"Une œuvre est . . . *toujours* une
œuvre collective . . ."   (Michel Butor)

Outside France, Michel Butor is still regarded primarily as a novelist, and one of the main aims of this study is to show that his activities in other domains are equally important, paralleling in many respects the most interesting developments in postwar musical theory and practice. I have also tried to establish the thematic coherence of an extremely diversified body of writings: essayist on literature, art, and music, creator of "mobile" texts, novelist, poet, collaborator in an experimental opera, Butor returns again and again to the same preoccupations, which form the substance of my first chapter. But because I am not certain what kind of relationship may safely be established between a writer's life and his work, I have normally refrained from searching for any so-called "links" between the two. On the other hand, *L'Univers imaginaire de Michel Butor* remains to be written by an apprentice Jean-Pierre Richard, and the reader will find some elements for such a study in the present text. Finally, I have expressed a number of reservations about Butor's work, and these may help to make my admiration more rather than less acceptable.

One advantage in writing on a living author—at least, when he is as well disposed as Michel Butor—is that he rapidly becomes a friend, and I have to thank the subject of my study for his unfailing courtesy and kindness. Other friends I have made in the course of writing the present book include Frederick St. Aubyn, of the University of Pittsburgh, Claude Senninger, of the University of New Mexico, and Jennifer Walters, of the University of Victoria, British Columbia, all of whom I thank for their encouragement and wish well in their own projects.

MICHAEL SPENCER

Monash University, Clayton,
Victoria 3168, Australia

Acknowledgments

I am grateful to Les Editions de Minuit, Editions Gallimard, Editions Bernard Grasset, and the Centre d'Etude et de Recherche Marxiste for permission to quote from works whose copyright they hold. I also wish to thank Simon and Schuster (New York) for permission to quote from the English translations of *Degrés* and *Mobile* published by them, and Henry Regnery Co. (New York) for permission to quote from the English translation of *6 810 000 Litres d'eau par seconde* published by them.

I am also grateful to the editorial board of *Essays in French Literature* for permission to reuse material originally published in that journal, No. 6, 1969, 81–101, and now forming the substance of my Chapter 3; to the *Australian Journal of French Studies* for permission to reuse material originally published in Vol. VI, 1969, 101–12, and now forming part of my Chapter 7 and other material of a bibliographical nature originally published in Vol. VIII, 1971, 84–97; and to the *Modern Language Review* for permission to reuse material originally published in Vol. LXIII, 1968, 57–65 and also forming part of my Chapter 7.

Some of my translations have been checked by M. Butor, who has suggested certain alterations; I should like to thank him for yet another manifestation of his generosity, although the final responsibility for interpretation and accuracy is, of course, my own.

Contents

Chronology

1926	Michel Butor born on September 14 at Mons-en-Barœul (Nord).
1929	Butor family moves to Paris.
1936– 1944	Various secondary schools, notably lycée Louis-le-Grand. Becomes interested in literature, painting, philosophy. Reads widely.
1944– 1949	Tertiary studies at Sorbonne. Obtains "licence de philosophie" but fails "agrégation." Meets many Surrealist writers and painters, notably André Breton and Jacques Hérold. Visits Germany on several occasions.
1950	Teaching post at Lycée de Sens. Fails "agrégation" again and accepts post as French teacher at El Minya (Upper Egypt), where he begins to write *Passage de Milan*.
1951– 1953	"Lecteur de français" at Manchester University, England.
1954	*Passage de Milan* published, almost unnoticed by critics and public. Accepts post at Lycée français de Salonique (Salonika, Greece). Begins *L'Emploi du temps*.
1956	*L'Emploi du temps* published. Post at Ecole internationale de Genève, where he meets his future wife, Marie-Jo.
1957	*La Modification*. Prix Théophraste-Renaudot.
1958	*Le Génie de lieu*. Marries Marie-Jo.
1959– 1960	Visiting Professor at Bryn Mawr, United States.
1960	*Répertoire; Degrés*.
1961	*Histoire extraordinaire, essai sur un rêve de Baudelaire*. Meets Henri Pousseur and begins work on *Votre Faust* (first performed January, 1969).
1962	*Mobile, étude pour une représentation des Etats-Unis; Réseau aérien* ("texte radiophonique").
1962– 1963	Visiting Professor at University of Buffalo, United States.
1963	*Description de San Marco*.
1964	*Répertoire II; Illustrations* (poems).
1965	Moves to Sainte-Geneviève-des-Bois, near Paris. *6 810 000 Litres d'eau par seconde* ("étude stéréophonique").
1966	Travels widely, notably to Japan, South Korea, and Cambodia (see *Où*).

1967	*Portrait de l'artiste en jeune singe* ("capriccio").
1968	*Répertoire III; Essais sur les Essais* (of Montaigne); *La Banlieue de l'aube à l'aurore, Mouvement brownien* (poems).
1969	*Illustrations II* (poems); *Les Mots dans la peinture.*
1969–1970	Visiting Professor, University of New Mexico, United States.
1970	*La Rose des vents, 32 rhumbs pour Charles Fourier.*
1971	Moves to Saint Laurent du Var, near Nice. Visits Australia and New Zealand. *Dialogue avec 33 variations de Ludwig van Beethoven sur une valse de Diabelli; Où, le génie du lieu, 2.*
1972	Moves to house overlooking the port at Nice. *Travaux d'approche* (poems). Establishment of "Fonds Michel Butor" at the Municipal library of Nice.
1973	*Intervalle, anecdote en expansion; Illustrations III.* "Approches de Michel Butor"—Colloquium held at the Centre Culturel International, Cerisy-la-Salle, France, June 24–July 1. Butor returns to New Mexico as visiting professor.

CHAPTER 1

Répertoire

1 *Literature and Utopia*

M ICHEL Butor is an unpretentious, hospitable family man in his mid-forties, who until recently divided most of his time between an outer suburban villa at Sainte-Geneviève-des-Bois and various American universities. He now lives at Nice. Courteous, punctual, a diligent correspondent whose letters and cards contrast in their simplicity with the complication of his published writings, M. Butor embodies many of the qualities one associates with the appellation "bourgeois." The gap between the author's aura of bourgeois respectability—mediocrity is a word one would never use—and his ceaseless written questioning of the traditional religious, social, and esthetic framework which many of us still accept, appears extremely wide. Butor partly bridged it himself in 1968, through his participation in the activities of the Union des écrivains, of which he was a founder member. Up to then, he had done no more than sign the usual protests against the wars in Algeria and Vietnam, while his written criticisms of the state of contemporary and past Western society had been indirect, sometimes extremely so, needing their own author or his most subtle commentators subsequently to uncover them. As late as 1964, the first monograph on Butor treated his works as interesting but largely gratuitous structural exercises.[1]

His part in the May events of 1968 should have suggested to the least sensitive of his readers that there might be more to his books than formal play. On May 21, 1968, Butor and about ten other writers, including Nathalie Sarraute and Jean-Pierre Faye, invaded—"very politely," according to *Le Monde*—the Hôtel de Massa, headquarters of the Société des gens de lettres. This venerable but useless body, founded in 1838, exercised a minimal influence on the nation's cultural life and was in no way representative of writers as a profession, as the invaders pointed out in a subsequent communiqué. In the same document, they announced

the formation of a "Union of writers . . . open to all who believe
that literary activity cannot be dissociated from the current revolutionary process."[2] The writer, stated Butor during one of the
confused debates following this action, "is always a challenger of
society."

On this occasion, the challenge was direct, even physical, reflected
in Butor's writing in the form of a political poem entitled "Tour-
mente."[3] But apart from this almost unique exception, his written
contestation remains what it has always been—oblique—relying
on a skilful manipulation of language and themes rather than any
attempt to prove a political or social thesis: Butor believes that
"littérature engagée" is largely a waste of time.[4] The notion of
literature as contestation is also what gives his work its seriousness
and urgency of tone, creating an extraordinary unity of preoccupation within a multiplicity of books and genres. There are exceptions,
of course, but the great majority of Butor's writings are based on
a violent personal reaction to what he sees as the *malaise* of the
Western world, stemming from the imposition of Christianity on a
way of life in direct contrast to it—with the blame falling on the
religion rather than on the society it has invaded. No particular
circumstance in his upbringing seems to be responsible for the
strength of this reaction, and I do not intend to search for one.
Nor does a knowledge of Butor's sources help very much; like
Gérard de Nerval, he appears to have read everything, although
with a far greater degree of critical awareness. And although certain
writers have clearly interested him, especially Joyce, Proust, Faulkner, Bachelard, Mallarmé, and Breton, the influence of none—with
the exception of the last two—has been strong or unique enough to
affect radically his outlook or technique, as opposed to confirming
theory and practice already established. Indeed, so genuine and
immediate is Butor's concern with our confusion that it would be
an insult to seek such "explanations"; reading him, I am ashamed
that we are all not concerned to the same extent.

Butor's first and third novels, *Passage de Milan* and *La Modification*, are in large part an allegorical description of our present spiritual plight, and many of the essays in the three volumes of *Répertoire* treat writers or artists whose awareness of it is reflected in their
work. The theme of "tearing" or "cracking," as Georges Raillard
has shown,[5] is a fundamental one in Butor, whose writings con-

stantly focus on moments in history or an individual's life when the clash of contradictory modes of thought, religious, mythical, or philosophical, is sharply felt. Writing in *Répertoire II*, Butor notes that:

> ... societies do not remain in isolation, they meet, make war or trade with one another, and it is not only their "real" elements that clash, are exchanged, arms or products, soldiers or merchants, but the imaginary elements, their gods.

Thus a certain amount of "play" between the sacred and the everyday will occur. The individual will rapidly experience "mythological confusion". He will no longer know precisely what are the important occasions, he will hesitate between two or three groups of holy days, temples, or priests; he will no longer know how to consecrate the key events of his own life, to which god to turn and devote himself.[6]

According to him, one of the many writers to experience this disorientation is Chateaubriand, who, sensitive to the "rending" of European society, "this cancer eating it away, ageing it, disturbing it, rotting it, making it opaque, the war between two contradictory value-systems, the 'Christian' and the 'Pagan' ...," sought in primitive America "a new cultural 'site' in which all traditions might unite, ceasing to tear at one another ..."[7] Although this "Fountain of Youth" was not to be found, at least Chateaubriand gained a perspective on our problems, providing an example that Butor has never forgotten on his regular visits to the United States. *Mobile* in particular is a meditation on the plight of the Western man, viewed from a country which, by its isolation from, and cultural kinks with Europe, tends to experience European contradictions even more violently than the continent from which they spring. For the same kind of reason, the presence of the *past* and the weight of our religious and cultural heritage is a frequent theme in Butor's work; the novel *La Modification* is a plea for our understanding of it and our subsequent emancipation from outdated religious and geographical concepts.

Other writers, deprived of Chateaubriand's external vantage point, are scrutinized by Butor for similar signs of "spiritual bewilderment." The methods of investigation used in James Joyce's *Ulysses* "make us feel that we are entering a crumbling world .... The intellectual worlds of Bloom and Stephen have

lost the support of certainty or transcendence, they are haunted by
the débris of the ancient systems.''[8] The aspect of John Donne's
work to which Butor is most sensitive is what he calls a kind of
sarcastic negation, a deliberate incongruity, a generalized questioning: "Donne saw himself as witness to a crumbling world . . ."[9]
In an article on the use of furniture in literature, he claims that
Balzac fills his houses with objects designed to symbolize "a totter-
ing society,"[10] while the theme of the giant in Rabelais is explained
in terms of the author's awareness of a contemporary world undergoing violent change.[11] Finally, Butor's theoretical articles are
filled with references to his—and our—generalized uncertainty and
disorientation.[12]

Spiritual war, deterioration, and change are thus the three
disturbing constants of Western society as Butor sees it. If this is
not already bad enough, our ability to achieve any kind of reconciliation between the conflicting beliefs that assail us is hampered by
the way in which we apprehend them. Butor believes that we do
not experience the outside world directly, but via a kind of fictional
and informational filter which interprets and distorts, while sepa-
rating us from it. Our life is dominated by the "récit," he writes,
not only in the restricted sense of a fictional story, but, more widely,
by any form of information: what we are taught at school or by
our parents, what we read in newspapers, hear on the radio, see
at the movies or on television.[13] For a cultured person, the novel
is one of his main sources of knowledge,[14] although Butor is very
aware of the recent changes in communication resulting from
developments in mass media.[15] More than ever, he believes,
our experience of the surrounding world—physical, cultural, social,
or philosophical—is secondhand, and our reactions to it are governed
by what others think about it. And in all cases, the "récit," fictional
or not, gives us a false picture: "The story gives us the world, but
it inevitably gives us a false world."[16] So our problem is now
twofold, since not only are we the focal point of contradictory
"systems" of all kinds, but the manner of their presentation is
inevitably distorted.

The falseness of the "récit" stems from a lack of synchrony
between language and the world it describes, with the former always
lagging behind the latter. Butor regards this state of affairs as
unavoidable: "it is the very structure of our society that causes

words constantly to lose their meaning, and us to be lost in the midst of words, because we lose our words."[17] The congruence between words and society is lost in a dual movement: words change their sense, sometimes losing their original meaning completely; at the same time, society changes even more rapidly, and we are faced with a situation where the loss of the words' original sense has not been offset by their development of a new meaning adequate to describe a vastly changed world. Any writer's first task is therefore to attempt a revitalization of language, which is the only means we have of coming to terms with our physical and mental environment.[18]

It is here that we encounter Butor's notion of "poetry," not as a refuge or a means of agreeably rhyming our thoughts, but as a systematic experimentation with language in order to restore its lost potentiality, enabling it not only to describe the world but to *transform* it. Butor gives succinct expression to this Surrealist concept of poetry in an essay on Ezra Pound, in which the notion of literature as contestation finds its clearest expression:

Pound is conscious to an extreme degree of the power and importance of poetry. For him, it is in no sense a distraction, just "literature," but an activity indispensable to the proper working of a society because it is the safeguard, the hygiene and the medicine of language.

Pound believes that words are deformed and diseased, that their relationship is a lie .... We must invent new means of expression in order to succeed in mastering the mental complexity in which we are struggling: the meeting, in our minds, of civilizations, their opposition and their mingling; in order to solve all of these problems, to find beyond them stable ground, truth, a reasonable society.

Given this state of affairs, the poet's activity is of necessity revolutionary.[19]

The "poet" here should be taken as any writer, practising any genre, who uses language in such a way as to bring about a transformation of society. Nor does Butor restrict the primacy of the means of expression to the literary domain. His increasing interest in painting involves close scrutiny of technique in order to discover if the artist concerned has evolved a new form of pictorial language translating his active dissatisfaction with the contemporary world. A brilliant essay on "Claude Monet ou le monde renversé," based on a series of metaphors—water as a symbol of the painter's activity, reflection implying transformation, interruption of perspective as a sign of aggressiveness toward the urban interiors in which his paintings hang—interprets what he calls the "dynamic instability" of Monet's subjects as a means of the artist saying: "The vision I am offering you is superior to the one with which we make do, my painting will change reality for you."[20] As usual, Butor is careful to support his assertions with a wealth of analytical detail, complementing in many respects more orthodox or technical approaches. More startling still, but even more indicative of the way his mind functions, is an essay on Mondrian which again emphasizes the relationship between paintings and the surroundings in which they are displayed. The fundamental problem faced by the modern painter, he writes, "is not only to denounce the disorder of contemporary reality by offering in its place the promise of harmonious future reality, but, through his painting, to begin constructing that reality."[21] In literature, painting—and, we shall see later, in music—the transformation of a chaotic present into a more harmonious future by their respective languages is a necessity.

In the realm of literature, the next problem is *how* to achieve the revitalization of language. Unfortunately, not only does Butor tell us relatively little, but his arguments sometimes appear vague and confused. The starting point is the author's division of French prosody into two categories, the "Classical," and the "Surrealist":

> The poet uses prosody, whether it be the Classical kind, which in France today means counting up to twelve, or the Surrealist kind, which means forming series of contrasting images; the poet invents by combining words within the framework of certain forms, by trying to organize them according to sonorous or visual requirements; thus he succeeds in rediscovering their meaning, in stripping them, in restoring their health, their active power.[22]

There are two key notions here: juxtaposition, or placing of words in apposition for their visual and alliterative[23] effect, and the use of structure, as a restraining framework. Elsewhere, Butor insists on the rigor of both procedures; the Surrealists' use of contrasting images creates, in his opinion, a prosody as strict as Boileau's,[24] while "the use of a rigorous form will enable us to trample on those dangerous tendencies of everyday language whereby words lose their meaning—words, things, events, laws."[25] As for the framework itself, it is not arbitrarily imposed, but partly determined by the form of reality to be examined; in the *Entretiens* with Georges Charbonnier, Butor talks in a quasi-scientific manner of the twofold relationship between the field of research (the aspect of reality to be examined) and the tool of discovery (the forms utilized), describing how each is modified by the other in a continuous process until a kind of compromise is reached (pp. 67–74).

In all this, the basic unit is the word, and its function one of relationship with others. The real confusion arises when, in the *Entretiens*, Butor stresses what could be called the "detergent" power of the writer:

when one cleanses language one cleanses it of its false poverty, of its acquired poverty. One cleanses it of the layer of dust that has accumulated, and which makes it one single color, an apparently, falsely simple color; after we have cleansed it we will rediscover its richness, its capacity for development.(p.245)

This is achieved, as has been suggested, by juxtaposition:

I put each word in the context of other words, these words being chosen so as to allow one another to develop what they are. (p. 20)

But what does Butor mean by "what they are" or, a little further on (p. 25) and elsewhere, the "lost meaning" of words? This seems to imply a fixed meaning, whereas elsewhere he speaks of their "richness" and "capacity for development"; a little after the last passage quoted, he describes the task as one of endowing the word with a new significance, thereby forcing the reader to examine it and rediscover the meaning of the words he frequently uses without knowing what they connote (p. 24). The confusion is only partly resolved a little later by the not unreasonable assertion that it is only by discovering what meaning words once possessed that we can endow them with a new one (p. 30).

In fact, both beliefs—in words as fixed, and words endowed with potentiality—while logically inconsistent with each other, are emotionally necessary to Butor, whose writings are haunted by Paradise Lost and informed by the desire to regain it by linguistic means. On the one hand, there is a bygone Golden Age, where harmony reigned between words and society,[26] on the other, there is a realization that, in a world which *becomes* rather than *is*, an equivalent state of harmony in the future can only be attained by a dynamic use of language, where the potentiality of words is their

most valuable feature. Butor himself never quite rationalizes this
far, although in a characteristically oracular passage he unites past
and future in terms of the *movement* of poetic thought, but not the
development of poetic language:

> This Golden Age can never be reconstructed at a precise point in the
> past . . . . The impulse of poetic thought, at first taking the form of a
> return towards a certain lost past, will be forced ever further back in time,
> so much so that it will only find rest outside the world and time, *anywhere*
> *out of the world* [Baudelaire], in a Utopia or a "uchronie" if you prefer, to
> use the term so aptly coined by the philosopher Renouvier, in that region
> outside history which will take the form of "what we desire." This reminis-
> cence and this nostalgia suddenly find their outlet in our future.
>
> Thus poetry, that critic of the present, proposes to change it.[27]

II *The Rôle of the Novel*

For several years, the novel was the main genre through which
Butor attempted his descriptive and transformational enterprise.
On a personal level, it became for him a means of reconciling two
previously incompatible preoccupations, poetry and philosophy,
while providing "a prodigious method of resisting, of continuing to
live intelligently" in the face of a hostile universe.[28] For Butor,
the novel should be an intermediary between the writer and the
outside world, not a fictional buffer filled by the products of his
imagination, but a "phenomenological" instrument for examining
what he experiences.[29] The novel, he writes, is different from other
forms of "récit" such as historical works or newspaper reports, in that
what it recounts is "unverifiable": for example, whatever an author
tells us about one of his characters can only be checked by reference
to the rest of his text. This is both obvious and reasonable, for even
if we discover that a fictional person is based on a real one, to accuse
the author of falsification if they do not correspond would be naïve
and fruitless, ignoring the special relationship between the novelist's
reality and outside reality. Butor illustrates this point in an essay on
"Balzac et la réalité,"[30] where he uses the image of two concentric
spheres to represent the novelist's fictional universe and the one in
which he actually lives. Their common center indicates that the one
can be discussed in terms of the other; indeed, an essential part of
all reading is a comparison of what the author tells us with what we

know, in order to decide its plausibility. Fiction and reality have a common structure, in the form of motivation, relationships within each, cause and effect, and so on. At the same time, fiction has an obvious autonomy deriving from the very existence of relationships within it: Goriot is plausible, not only because we way have met or heard of someone like him in real life, but because, within the novel, he is a lonely man with two rich daughters.

But Butor goes beyond this elementary point, in reversing the usual relationship between the novel and reality, where the latter has precedence. He does this by insisting on the importance of formal research within the novel, which will allow it to develop the powers normally associated with "poetry":

By broadening the meaning of the word style—which is essential in view of the experience of the modern novel—by generalizing it, by taking it on all levels, it is easy to show that, by using sufficiently powerful structures, comparable to those of verse, comparable to geometric or musical structures, by systematically putting the elements into reciprocal relationship until they finally produce that revelation which the poet expects from his prosody, one can integrate totally, in the context of a description whose starting-point is utter banality, the powers of poetry.[31]

And "poetry," we have seen, is synonymous with transformation. The novel, by utilizing new means of structuring information, will alter our perception, since it is one of the main ways in which the world is filtered for us. And if the world is perceived differently, it becomes different, and is thus transformed:

as soon as the novel has succeeded in imposing itself as a new language . . . a new way of linking information chosen as examples, as a means of showing us how to retain the information that concerns us, it will proclaim its difference from what is said every day, and will appear as poetry. . . .

. . . all great works . . . transform the way in which we see and recount the world, and consequently transform the world.[32]

Only the last link is perhaps not clear, and to explain it we must return to the word "phenomenology." Of all the practitioners of the "nouveau roman," Butor has undoubtedly the best knowledge of philosophy and particularly of the phenomenological movement. Nevertheless, it would be wrong to look for an application of any philosophical "system" in his writings. It would be particularly wrong where phenomenology is concerned, since it is at its best as a "style" of thought and not as a system. But there are definite similarities between the phenomenological outlook and Butor's novelistic practice, notably in the treatment of the human consciousness and the rôle of objects. For the phenomenologist, man and the world are inextricably linked, with the one implying the other.[33] In Butor's case, this special relationship between man and the outside world is true of all his novels, and particularly *La Modification* (see Chapter 4). The protagonist's consciousness cannot be treated separately from the world, since its only mode of being is one of a relationship with that world, which it "intends": it is always a consciousness of something. The objects in Léon Delmont's railway compartment (*La Modification*) are all important as objects of his perception, not just as parts of a realistic décor.[34] Similarly, the "reality" of the compartment is not just the presence of its constituent parts (the Sartrian "en-soi"), but the interaction between them and the subjectivity regarding them whereby the consciousness both modifies, and is modified by, its surroundings. The compartment retains its physical presence, unalterable in this respect. But for Delmont, as for us, it has nevertheless changed. No longer just a railway compartment, it is the meeting ground for memories, dreams, day dreams, hallucinations, and thoughts of the future. In an essay on "L'Espace du roman," Butor writes:

Space as experienced by us is not at all the Euclidean space whose parts are mutually exclusive. Every place is the focal point of a horizon of other places, the point of origin of a series of possible routes passing through other more or less determined regions.

In my town many other towns are present through a variety of intermediaries: direction signs, geography books, things coming from them, newspapers talking about them, pictures and movies which show them to me, my memories of them, novels which make me pass through them.[35]

The "site," whether town (*L'Emploi du temps*), railway compartment, apartment block (*Passage de Milan*), or classroom (*Degrés*), is thus transformed by our manner of perceiving it, in which the whole of our mental life is involved. For in Butor's opinion, the research function of the novel is hampered if it concentrates solely on the externals of our behavior. An essential part of any society, we have already seen, is its "mythology," or the total of its beliefs; where they play their rôle properly, society will be har-

monious yet primitive, he claims.[36] But what usually happens is
that the "mythological" world is full of contradictions, with disastrous consequences for us all. For this main reason,[37] Butor is not
particularly interested in analyzing what is normally considered to
be "psychological" man, the "hero," as he appears in the novels of
Stendhal, for instance. The protagonist is unimportant alongside
what he represents; through him, especially his dreams or mythical
affiliations, Butor seeks partial illumination of mankind's behavior
in a world full of mystery. Again, we are reminded of Surrealism:
"Within Surrealism there is Realism .... There can be no true
realism unless one allows imagination its share, unless one under-
stands that the imaginary is within the real, and that we see reality
through it. A description of the world which did not take account
of the fact that we dream would be but a dream."[38] Just as it is
possible to discover the universality of the *Odyssey* in the heart of
twentieth-century Dublin,[39] similarly Butor's novels make considerable use of dreams and mythological symbolism in order to
uncover some kind of pattern or structure underlying our acts.
Although we know virtually nothing about Jacques Revel's character in *L'Emploi du temps*, his behavior in the midst of the
malefic city of Bleston is clarified by reference to three mythical
figures, Œdipus, Theseus, and Cain; Léon Delmont's dreams, in
some of which he plays the part of Æneas, or encounters the
"Great Huntsman," indicate his disorientation and enable it to
be related to his persistence in accepting the myth of Rome as the
center of man's spiritual universe; the abbé Jean Ralon's dreams
in *Passage de Milan* show clearly his dilemma—and that of modern Western man—as the focal point of conflicting ethical systems.
Butor and—less successfully—his heroes attempt to reduce chaos
to order by inventing a network of symbols by which nothing less
than our destiny is implied.

The novel was, until 1960, the most successful means Butor
had so far devised of achieving some kind of unity in his own life
and of structuring and transforming reality itself. With these aims,
it is not surprising that it is essentially experimental and also highly
self-conscious. According to Butor, the novelist, as his own and
first reader, should be constantly interrogating himself, his self-
questioning forming a reply to the changing image of the world
and being reflected within the novel as in a mirror.[40] His novels

are thus full of people discussing the novel or trying to write in a variety of genres (with remarkably little success), both activities playing an important part in the parent or "outer" book's symbolism. While there is nothing particularly new in this, particularly after Gide's *Les Faux-Monnayeurs*, Butor and his protagonists have slightly different terms of reference. The question is no longer: what is the relationship of the novel to the reality it purports to describe? but: what is its relationship to the reality it intends to *change*? This point seems to be neglected by certain recent critics of Butor or theoricians of the "new novel," for whom, in Jean Ricardou's words, the essential process is the "adventure of writing,"[41] or, to put it unkindly, a series of futile generative exercises. Similarly, for a recent writer to sum up the deeper significance of *Passage de Milan* as "an involved allegory of the conditions under which a novel comes into existence and the way it must be organized by the novelist"[42] is seriously to underestimate the moralistic implications which he himself stresses a few pages later. While the reflection on form within the novel is undoubtedly an essential part of the novel, as Butor conceives it, the presence of certain themes to which that form is appropriate is the *sine qua non* of its own existence.

III   *Mobility and Openness*

Around 1962 a further development in Butor's thought became apparent, with the concept of "mobility" assuming great importance, possibly as a result of his friendship with Henri Pousseur, possibly even because of his knowledge of Umberto Eco's researches in the domain of the "open" work. Eco had had discussions with Pousseur on modern music, and the latter may therefore have acted as a kind of intellectual intermediary between the theorician and the practician.[43] Basically, he seems to have decided that the novel, in spite of its structural advantages, was not a sufficiently flexible form to translate the complication of the modern world-in-flux. Although chaos should not be submitted to, the opposite danger of a "fixed" representation of mobile reality was one which his protagonists had failed to avoid, and which Butor felt that he risked. *Mobile*, his first systematic application of the theory of mobility, is surrounded, chronologically, by a whole cluster of essays treating the topic exclusively or in part. The feature common to all is a treatment of the book as a flexible medium through which material can be presented *simultaneously* as well as *successively*:

> The book, as we understand it today, is ... the arrangement of the thread of the story within a three-dimensional space, according to a double measure: length of line, depth of page, an arrangement which has the advantage of allowing the reader great freedom of movement in relation to the "unfolding" of the text, a great mobility, an arrangement which is the closest there is to a simultaneous presentation of all parts of a work.[44]

In other words, not only can the page be utilized with great freedom, but the third dimension of the book—its thickness, formed of instantly separable pages—allows a further degree of freedom. The book is an object-to-be-flicked-through.[45]

By availing himself of every resource of the "book as object," Butor has gained enormously in flexibility. If the "reality" of the United States, or, in later works, Niagara Falls or St. Mark's, Venice, is the sum of the continually altering relationships between its constituent parts, these are better translated in a "mobile" fictional work, and particularly by the use of juxtaposition within it. Its structure is no less carefully planned than that of the novels, but it is so devised as to allow the reader more freedom of choice than previously: he is invited, by the text's very form, to select or suppress material from it, according to his own wishes, certain "rules," or a combination of both. In *Mobile*, the reader has a free hand; in *6 810 000 Litres d'eau par seconde*, certain itineraries are proposed, to be combined at his will; in *Votre Faust*, the audience can vote or intervene in order to determine the course of the action. This does not imply an abnegation of responsibility on Butor's part, since each work is composed of a limited number of elements, chosen and organized according to his own subjective interests. But it does allow the reader to complement the author's freedom and responsibility by his own exploitation of the possibilities within the text. There is of course always a gap between an author's intentions and the reader's response, and it would be very wrong to suggest that Butor had invented "active" reading.[46] Nevertheless, the structures employed make the gap wider, and in all of the "mobile" works there is a point where Butor appears deliberately to relinquish control, and the play of chance, or "'deliberate' chance" as Eco puts it (p. 160), seems to be invited.

In a brief but masterly article, Jean Roudaut has examined Butor's debt to the author of *Un Coup de dés*,[47] in respect of the concept of mobility, the "book as object," reader participation, a general preoccupation with language, and formal research. Above all, he explains, the problem of chance exercises both authors. Exegetes of Mallarmé would all agree that chance cannot be abolished, but differ as to the repercussions of this negative. In Butor's case, his "mobile" texts are so designed that chance is *controlled*, or "caressed," as he picturesquely put it at a press conference in Milan at the time of the premiere of *Votre Faust*. A text should be "unfinished" or "open" in Butor's terms, just as a piece of music should be "overdetermined" in Pousseur's, combining rigidity and variability, needing the reader-critic as a collaborator whose rôle is as important as the author's.

Two relatively early essays on Hugo—yet another "traditional" author whom Butor admires[48]—enable us to unravel this complicated series of claims. Both pieces celebrate the potentiality of the "open" book in oracular terms, while using the image of the library-prison to denounce the harmful effects of the "closed" text. Butor sees the intellectual and spiritual history of mankind as resumed in a series of books, gradually piled on top of one another, no longer protecting us against the menace of the outside world, but constituting a monument that is turned oppressively inward rather than defensively outward. Each book's message appears out of date; it is no longer read, but its authority or *weight* prevents more recent ones from being opened. The function of the new book must therefore be a liberating one: "The book-monument of today must restore to previous ones their transparency, their lost presence, it must force us to read them. . . ."[49] But how much easier its task would be if the myth of a book's authority or definitiveness were dispelled, and authors no longer imagined that their products constituted a final word on any matter. For while any book, by virtue of its situation in time, will tend to become "closed" (i.e., its potentiality is exhausted), there are also many that are "closed" as soon as they are written, their pseudo-completeness rendering them an obstacle to progress and sterile in themselves. These Butor scornfully denounces as "masques," "façades," or "apocryphes."[50] The "true" book, on the other hand, is "ruin, dilapidation leading to discovery,"[51] a work whose very incompleteness symbolizes its potentiality. Two of Butor's novels, *L'Emploi du temps* and *Degrés*, are parables on this theme, demonstrating the importance of the unfinished book and the paradox of its fictional author's "failure," which is really a success.

The "true" book is normally not a ruin, however, but merely "unfinished," in the sense that its author knows that he can never provide a definitive interpretation of his field of study. The reader's rôle, never inconsiderable,[52] is greatly increased if the book is a consciously *provisional* and *open* construct. Perhaps the best analogy is with serialist music, and both Butor and Pousseur have employed it, the former in connection with Boulez' "Improvisations,"[53] the latter when describing the music of Webern, which "no longer possesses the thematic rigidity of the series of Schoenberg" but has "a structure within which—without the over-all coherence of the work being put in danger—there is a true mobility." This is achieved because the strict ordering element (the series of twelve tones) still leaves the piece with autonomy: "It is, then, not *indetermined*, but rather *indeterminable*, for the simple reason that it is too rich and too pregnant to be categorized by a single definition or characterization. It is thus literally *overdetermined.* ... "[54] In this way, chance is an integral and definable element in a musical work, the dimension within which the musician can operate with far greater freedom of interpretation than he had hitherto. Similarly, the reader of *Mobile* or the spectator of *Votre Faust* has a choice—and a responsibility—which give the word collaboration a very real meaning. His reaction and choice cannot be predicted, but there is still an over-all term of reference within which he must operate—in a very active sense.

For Butor's ideal reader is, it has already been hinted, a critic, not in any narrowly professional sense, but a being whose chief function is to compare the book he reads with others, contemporary or past, and in turn relate these to the world in which he lives. Reading is essentially a rewriting in terms of one's own experience,[55] the filling of gaps deliberately or unconsciously left by the author, just as the "creative" act is initially a response to the fact that "there is something lacking," that a region of reality has not been properly explored, usually because the right instruments have been lacking.[56] Those readers who actively rewrite by subse-

quently becoming what is normally meant by a critic, help replace
the library-prison by an "open" edifice, formed by a proliferation
of texts, "creative" and "critical," whose form is dictated by
reference to each other and the reality they respond to and try to
change:

> Critical activity implies the consideration of works as unfinished, poetic
> activity, "inspiration" presents reality itself as unfinished.
> Functionally.
> Each time an original work, invention, exists, however gratuitous it may
> seem on first acquaintance, we gradually feel the necessity to use it as a
> basis for rearranging the world to which we belong.
> Every work is 'engagée', even the most humdrum, since every activity
> of the mind has a function in society; the more profoundly inventive it is,
> the more it provokes change.[57]

The ideal writer thus emerges as a humble person, who realizes
that his personality is of little importance alongside the society
his works describe.[58] He is no longer the creative genius to be
admired, but a man whose work—as always—belongs to the
public domain once it is issued, although its value is to be judged
by rather unusual criteria. It will be most successful if—rather like
a crystal around which others cluster—it becomes the center of a
ramification of texts preparing the future and illuminating the
past.[59] Its main function is thus generative, with its ultimate term
of reference reality, and never the personality of its creator. Judged
by normal psychological terms, Butor's protagonists are shadowy
people, what they stand for being more important than what they
are. Again, while his own subjectivity is responsible for the published text, he clearly sees this as an unfortunate but inevitable
fact, seeking to diminish the effect of his personality by demanding
the collaboration of his readers. From here, it is but a small step
to the *initial* complementing of our subjectivity by others', in the
form of a collective work.

It took Butor sixteen years to bridge the gap between theory
and practice in this unusual aim. One of his earliest essays, a
piece on science-fiction published in 1953, proposes a collective
science-fiction novel which, he claims, will exercise as much power
over the individual's imagination as anything from classical mythology.[60] In his first novel, *Passage de Milan*, a group of writers
are trying to compose a collective work, with little success and a

great deal of contradictory theoretical chatter. But in the last four years, *Votre Faust* and a number of the review *L'Arc* are an imperfect but practical application of the views he has expressed in theory and debated in fictional form. The "variable" opera is of course still a long way removed from the ideal of widespread initial collaboration, since it is the product of only two men. Nevertheless, as I have attempted to show in Chapter 7, the usual demarcation line between librettist and composer is never adhered to, with every aspect of the work owing a great deal to Butor and Pousseur. *L'Arc* is very unlike the usual "special" number of a review, where a number of experts treat a common theme or author, and much closer to a *Festschrift*, except that Butor himself contributes, organizing "a structure within which other writers could introduce their improvisations"—an excellent example of the principle of the "open" work.

Certain subjects which Butor has been unable to treat will be developed, he explains—not, however, as if he were writing them himself: "the introduction of their voices in the piece must finally appear as the best way I had of writing it." For, as he writes elsewhere, "each of us leaves a profound mark on his fellow-contributor": ideally, a work in collaboration should allow this reciprocal influence to occur, allowing what he calls a "common originality" to develop.[61] *L'Arc* has not been particularly successful in this respect, as many of the contributors have simply aped Butor's "mobile" technique. In other words, the influence appears to be all one way, and instead of a common originality one has a succession of pastiches of Butor. However, it is a most important development, and we may well see a succession of more ambitious and more successful works in collaboration in the next few years, with Butor as principal organizer. In the interview serving as introduction to *L'Arc*, he speaks of a long-standing desire to write "a novelistic (or quasi-novelistic) work within which I would have asked certain friends to write certain passages" (p. 4). If Butor's university commitments allow him time to realize this dream, it will be yet another challenge to convention by one of the most ambitious—and modest—writers of our time.

IV   *Science and Surrealism*

Many of the ideas outlined so far will seem at first strange, even irrelevant, to the American reader. When looked at closely, however, they nearly all turn out to be ingenious extensions of accepted commonplaces. Few people if any would question the claim that a major function of "poetic" language is the enrichment of our imagination, that any worthwhile reading entails mental rewriting, or that we are surrounded by an informational network that filters knowledge. Butor's originality is to have pushed these and other ideas to the limit and then combined them in a remarkably coherent fashion. Having said this, I must immediately qualify it, in order to correct an impression of Butor that may have been fostered by this chapter.

The *Entretiens*, or the more technical pieces in the three volumes of *Répertoire*, sometimes read like the observations of an eccentric research scientist or geometrician who has strayed into the realm of literature. Mr. John Sturrock, in an excellent study of Butor and two other "new novelists," Claude Simon and Alain Robbe-Grillet, calls him "by far the most dauntingly cerebral" of all three.[62] Butor is an exceptionally widely read man with a sound knowledge of mathematics and philosophy, and a mind versed in these disciplines may well find him immediately on its wavelength. But for those of us who are not mathematicians or philosophers, Butor's work may be saved from arid intellectualism—and appear most human—by virtue of the very unreasonableness of some of his claims and preoccupations. There is something engagingly naïve in the vastness of his enterprise and his frank Utopianism, the complementing of science by myth and dreams, or the enormous claims for language, all of which mark him as a descendant of the Surrealists.[63] It is because the Surrealist or Romantic in Butor guides the researcher that his writings are alive with an intensity and humor which render their fundamental seriousness acceptable on a human level, whatever reservations one may have about their objective validity. The discernment of these qualities is one of the many tasks of the chapters to follow.

CHAPTER 2

Passage de Milan

I *Cards and Counterpoint*

BUTOR'S "autobiography," *Portrait de l'artiste en jeune singe*,[1] is unusual in two major respects. Although based on a real trip to Germany in 1950, it is less a retrospective account of what happened than a (re)construction of his main interests at that time and a construction of his dreams.[2] Another curious feature is the contrast and interaction between the author's nocturnal and diurnal selves: on the one hand, the conscious Butor then, as now, fascinated by alchemy, the occult, and above all, what he later described in an interview as "our profound link with the Middle Ages";[3] on the other, the dreaming Butor—not the least important by any means—reliving the adventures of a young man from the *Arabian Nights*.[4] In fact, Butor's Germany, rather like that of Gérard de Nerval, turns out to be no more than a geographic and cultural staging-post on the "voyage en orient" undertaken by so many writers of an essentially Romantic temperament. For the journey in space to Germany, and in time to the Middle Ages, still took place within the confines of Western European civilization, and as such provided an insufficient answer to the author's literal and figurative *disorientation*. That he felt keenly at the time the need for an external reference point, which paradoxically would only increase his uncertainty, is indicated by his haste in accepting, on his return to France, a post as French teacher in the small Egyptian town of El Minya. It was here that *Passage de Milan* was begun, although it was not to be published until 1954, by Les Editions de Minuit.

While engaged in his not overarduous teaching duties, Butor had ample time to observe the town and its inhabitants, particularly his own pupils. Their disorientation was, to his horror, even greater than his own, he notes in the essay on Egypt forming part of *Le Génie du lieu* (Grasset, 1958). Caught between the vestiges of a past in which they only half-believed—the Pharaonic and Islamic traditions of their own country—and the influx of European culture, with its Christian substructure, their "chaotic mental vacuum" (p. 156) was in urgent need of a new historical perspective, he wrote. Our own Western one was clearly inadequate: "Now what can be called standard European thought . . . really could not help the Egyptians in this respect, nor can it still.

"For if it demands a certain type of historical perspective, the one it puts forward possesses insufficient temporal and geographic dimensions" (p. 191). For the Egyptian peasant, as well as ourselves, he concludes, a comparative revaluation of both Western and Oriental history becomes vitally necessary, a task entailing immense changes in emphasis and perspective (pp. 191–94). Visiting historical sites thus meant for Butor far more than the usual touristic ritual: at Saqqarah, El Amarna, and particularly Luxor, he sought "a renewal, a better means of defining problems which had been bothering me for years and which, on the site, bothered me more directly and more deeply" (p. 196).

No proper answer was forthcoming. A chance encounter at Luxor with an Egyptian peasant he had met on the boat transporting him from Marseille, provided at most a brief, slightly ludicrous interlude of mutual though dumb understanding between the representatives of two diverse cultures, in the form of a "slide-evening" of the peasant's views of Paris. The essay ends on a note of lucid despair and nostalgia:

> And I knew full well that this understanding between us, so solid, so pure, yet dumb, needed something if it were to become a spoken understanding, a true conversation: an organization, already in existence, to which we could refer, on which we could count, a satisfactory organization of those various sites and moments that the present moment brought together (pp. 208–9).
>
> When shall I return to Egypt? (p. 210)

Even if, typically, Butor can do no more than suggest a tentative answer, the problem is clearly posed: modern man is culturally, historically, and spiritually lost in the midst of a rapidly changing world. How can we improve this state of affairs without denying our rich yet bewildering heritage? The solution appears to be some kind of reconciliation—and organization—of the maximum amount of obviously contradictory knowledge, without thereby inhibiting the process of historical development and change. Or, in the terminology of Butor and his French critics, the "clôture" of a decrepit system must be superseded by an "open," fluid one. It is in the light of this question and possible answer that *Passage de Milan*, indeed the whole of Butor's work, must be examined.

The surface appeal of the novel is very slight. Briefly, it treats, in twelve sections, twelve hours in the lives of several families inhabiting an anonymous but very Parisian apartment block, demonstrating how individual destinies affect each other, and culminating in the apparently accidental death of a young girl. A fairly broad cross-section of Parisian society is portrayed, from the concierges on the ground floor to an orphan, a slightly deranged old lady and an "employé de métro"[5] whose means only permit them to lodge immediately under the roof. Two floors below, the upper middle classes are represented in pretention rather than fact by the Vertigues family, while the upper class is obviously absent from a rather seedy building. No one individual stands out as exceptional or even memorable, although many have an important rôle in the novel's rather heavy symbolic structure.[6]

As well as a good deal of movement between floors—many of the inhabitants, as well as outside guests, are invited to the twentieth birthday dance of M. and Mme Vertigues' only daughter, Angèle—three other families receive external visitors. The Mognes, who live on the third floor, are entertaining their eldest daughter, Jeanne, and her husband, Henri, at a rather crowded supper (there are two grandparents, two other daughters, and three sons). Samuel Léonard, a bachelor on the floor above, is holding a discussion evening on the future of the prophetic novel. On the sixth floor, the painter Martin de Vere has a small group of friends in. Apart from discussion and movement, the only event is nevertheless a dramatic one; one of the Vertigues' guests, Henri Delétang, has hidden in the cellar until the others have left, with the intention of returning to steal what he can conveniently carry off. Surprised by Angèle, he tries to kiss her; Louis Lécuyer, the orphan from the seventh floor, hears her cry, rushes down and hurls a candle holder at Henri. Angèle slips and strikes her temple against the marble edge of the fireplace, dying instantaneously. Louis hides in the cellar, where he is found by Samuel Léonard and persuaded to flee to Egypt. Neither the death nor Louis' subsequent flight are very plausible, and I shall return to this point later.

Passage de Milan opens at 7:00 P.M., with the abbé Jean Ralon leaning out of his second-floor window to gaze at the sordid view:

> The abbé Ralon leant out of his window. The whole of Paris surrounded him, separated by a false wall of fog and smoke, the color of tincture of iodine, chestnuts, and old wine, beyond an apparently empty, vague, open space (apart from two scrawny yet somehow elegant trees that already had a few leaves, enclosed by fences covered in posters), where, looking closely, one could see worn boards, thick planks, battens, then stones, old iron, material that could no longer be used, one might think, slowly polished by the wind alone, eaten away by the dust alone. And yet the squalid mass was constantly being stirred by eddies. (p. 7)

With the exception of the last sentence, the passage is largely a poetic introduction to one of the novel's main themes—decay. A heterogeneous collection of abandoned, apparently useless leftovers of modern urban civilization, set in an atmosphere of smoke and haze,[7] the objects lie for month after month, surrounding the building, itself insecurely constructed on the crypt of a church, and continually shaken by the metro.[8] "Supposing it collapsed one day . . . [*sic*]," thinks Henri Delétang, hiding in the cellar, a remark which, in the context of the novel, clearly refers not only to the "immeuble" but also to the Christian faith (p. 213). Within the building, few rooms show no sign of a similar decrepitude: a ceiling bulb in the de Vere's apartment has been smashed (p. 74); one of the four bulbs of the Mognes' electrolier is missing (p. 76); the walls of the Ralons' apartment are yellow and filthy, the books' covers in shreds (p. 97); Martin de Vere's unfinished painting is ruined by fire (p. 262).

Many of the novel's unimpressive characters live on a diet of memory, regret, and discontent. Frédéric Mogne (the Léon Delmont of *La Modification* ten years older?) presides over an archetypal "famille nombreuse" in feeble and disgruntled fashion and complains of his wretched job (p. 12). The lot of the surviving grandparents, Paul Mogne and Marie Mérédat, is the usual unhappy one. Tolerated rather than respected, they are fed but barely spoken to; the latter in particular falls back on memories for the consolation—and regret—they provide (pp. 127–28). Virginie Ralon and her cook, Charlotte Tenant, vie in cherishing the memory of the same man, their respective husband and lover, long since dead.[9] Virginie's son, the abbé Alexis, a failed schoolteacher in his own

eyes,[10] tormented by unchaste nightmares (p. 185), regrets above
all his lost opportunity to travel (*ibid.*). His brother Jean has lost
his faith (p. 283) and at the end of the novel is in despair. In lighter
vein, M. Vertigues fights off thoughts of creeping old age by putting
on his "pyjama de séducteur" (p. 186). The past weighs heavily
on many characters, but they appear to have learned nothing from
it. Trapped by it, their jobs, and a decaying building, their own
façade is gradually stripped during the night: Vincent Mogne is
revealed as having a homosexual relationship with Samuel Léonard's
Egyptian boy, Ahmed, while Alexis Ralon's affection for his
nephew, Louis, is of a similar nature but kept in check by his conscience. Henri Delétang has come to Angèle's party for the sole
purpose of stealing; another guest turns out to be the mistress of
one of the tenants, Gaston Mourre. There is no moralizing intention
here on the part of Butor, simply an indication of the *fissures*[11]
present in an apparently stable society.

Memories and reminders of an entirely different culture introduce
a further unsettling element. Ahmed, nostalgic for his native land,
remembers the last kites he had seen at Alexandria (p. 239), and the
"cruel race of birds" (p. 57) haunts the building and its inhabitants:
hovering above the waste area as Jean Ralon looks out of his
window is a kite (p. 8). *Passage de Milan*, a typically Butorian play
on words, indicates not only the narrow street in which the apartment block is situated but also the savage visit of a bird of prey,
the penetration of society by a hostile and exotic element.[12] Ahmed's
master, "the self-important gentlemen on the third floor, bachelor,
collector, back from the East . . . [*sic*]" (p. 30), inhabits a kind of
Egypto-Persian museum (pp. 67–68), whose carpet has birds as one
of its principal motifs (p. 276).

But the focal point of the East's "presence" is the doubting priest,
Jean Ralon. Fascinated yet profoundly disturbed by the perpetuation of ancient Middle Eastern civilizations, he ultimately rejects
the Catholic faith for the same basic reason as Léon Delmont in
La Modification. No religious or other "system" can withstand the
continual process of historical change, deny totally the system preceding it, or close its eyes to the implications of other contemporary
modes of thought, although the Roman Catholic church has struggled
to with more perseverance than other religious bodies. Whereas
Delmont realizes at the end of his journey to Rome that the notion

of the Eternal City as unique geographic-religious center of the world no longer corresponds to contemporary reality, Jean Ralon is tortured by the awareness that his faith has failed to exorcise the ancient gods who crowd his mental universe. Feelings of guilt inhibit any syncretic attempt to reconcile opposing systems, and the abbé, following a series of dreams in which he goes through the Egyptian *Tuat*, or underworld,[13] only to be excluded from the realm of light, can do no more than lament his loss of faith and blame Christ for his present state: "Why have you handed me over to these enchanters of old who laugh at my ignorance? I accuse you: I was bound to you for ever, and now, in spite of myself, wherever I turn, I am inevitably an apostate" (p. 284).

Passage de Milan has at first sight little to offer in the way of consolation or hope, and in this respect is typical of Butor's novels. Léon Delmont abandons his mistress and possible rejuvenation for a life of misery with his wife; the hero of *L'Emploi du temps* fails to "catch up with himself" in writing his diary and loses both women he might have married; Pierre Vernier's enterprise in *Degrés* literally kills him. Here, the book's amalgam of sordidness, violence, regret, and loss of faith is only occasionally relieved by humor. Nevertheless, there are three people who have not been completely submerged by the tides of conflicting civilizations: the painter Martin de Vere (Butor's Elstir), the Egyptologist Samuel Léonard, and the author himself.

De Vere's[14] "*unfinished* painting" (p. 111, my italics) is at once a "study for a representation" of the structure and content of Butor's novel and, in its initially unfinished and later flawed states, an indication of a possible solution to the problem outlined at the beginning of this chapter. It consists of twelve squares disposed in three rows of four, each one containing groups of representations of objects (cards), themselves performing the function of signs or symbols. The standard pack is used, distributed four to a square in the top and bottom rows, and five to a square in the middle one (pp. 111–19). Several very obvious parallels with *Passage de Milan* can be drawn and are made explicit later on: the twelve squares of the painting, which the artist constantly refers to as a "house," symbolize the twelve divisions of Butor's novel, each one inhabited by numerous figures who, in their turn, have a symbolic part to play. If one omits the three de Vere children, who never speak, the "employé de métro" who is out, and the two concierges, there are twenty-six inhabitants and twenty-seven external guests. It is tempting to equate the superfluous figure with the "annoying queen" (p. 121: Angèle Vertigues) of the painting, facing the Knave of Clubs (the jealous Louis Lécuyer) but separated from him by the Ace of Spades (Henri Delétang, who separates Louis and Angèle definitively by precipitating her death). At all events, de Vere's dilemma as to how to fit this "annoying queen" into his pictorial scheme, and the suggestion of a guest: "Why not just get rid of her?" (*ibid.*) is a clear prefiguration of Angèle's death, made even more obvious when the painting catches fire and melts in the center—at the very end of the novel's sixth chapter (p. 180). In case the reader has missed the card symbolism, Butor rather irritatingly allows a guest of the Vertigues, Bénédicte, to refer to Angèle and the Mogne brothers as "the Queen of Hearts" and "the Knaves" (p. 170).

But the principal and more subtle analogy is with music. According to Henri Pousseur in an interview, the method of composition de Vere adopts for his paintings is basically the same as that used in composing serialist music.[15] Within the novel itself, there are several occasions on which they are described in musical terms: the squares of the "unfinished painting" are likened to Gregorian notes (p. 113), while its present starkness is defended as forming the rhythmic base on which melodic invention will then be superimposed (p. 84). This series of musical references appears to be an attempt by Butor to defend his own method of composing the novel. The night's activities are centered around the "heroine," Angèle, for whom a dance is being given. However, around her there is not only a literal gyration of the invited couples, but a figurative one of the many other people who are indirectly affected by, or involved in, her fate. Within the "immeuble" and the architecture of the novel describing it, an immense counterpoint of figures and scenes is set up, in which inhabitants and guests move between floors, meet, visit, and avoid one another, or are contrasted by their thoughts. Speaking of the development of his painting, de Vere explains: "The lines soon intersected, I multiplied the basic forms and invented laws governing their meeting .." (*sic*, p. 113). Although I have been unable to discover the laws governing the juxtaposition of characters and scenes within *Passage de Milan*—although I suspect that the game of "patience" would supply it—the principle of rigidity of framework (the twelve sections) and, within it, variety of combination, is already present, pointing the way to the organization, on a mathematical or musical basis, of Butor's later works.

De Vere's painting is eventually ruined by fire, to his despair. Meanwhile a whole group of writers in the same building is engaged on a similarly ambitious but no more fruitful enterprise. There is something gratuitous about de Vere's efforts; he appears obsessed by technique, with nothing very much to express. On the contrary, Léon Wlucky, Jacques Vimaud, Antonin Creil, and the other writers gathered in Samuel Léonard's apartment have a surfeit of ideas but little interest in the detail of their presentation, and their long, confused and obscure arguments have an air of touching absurdity. Most are trying to write prophetic works, but, as their host sorrowfully observes, with every hour they are refuted (p. 143). One appears to have tried to cheat by writing a "histoire anticipée" in which the hero, an archaeologist from the future, discovers certain hieroglyphic or cuneiform inscriptions which at once confirm and invalidate many of our beliefs. But he has abandoned his task (p. 146). The weight of the past is one of the principal embarrassments. Should one try to ignore it, as one speaker suggests, by suppressing all memory in one's fictional characters?— "But they will have forgotten everything about us and our history. In what respect can we consider them as our future?"—objects another (p. 180). In any case, someone else maintains, prophetic works, especially of a scientific nature, often read paradoxically as if they described an ancient past (pp. 182–83).

Nevertheless, the attempt is still worthwhile: " . . . if waking man had to deny his consciousness even projects for improvement, sleep would take its revenge" (p. 153). It is Samuel Léonard who suggests a solution similar to one proposed by Butor in his essay on science-fiction published the previous year: a collective work of art, drawing on and synthesizing the ideas of many contributors (pp. 205–7). At this point, the conversation peters out, with Léonard and his friends joining the other Butorian protagonists who engage in debate, sometimes begin writing, but presumably never finish their project. On an exemplary level, their discussion is of obvious importance, since Butor himself has moved toward the ideal of a collective work. What is curious, but not confined to this novel, is the introduction of a protagonist whose views agree broadly with Butor's, but who is prevented by the author from carrying them out. The obvious parallel is with Gide's *Les Faux-Monnayeurs*, where Uncle Edouard is at once a spokesman for his creator and a rather feeble being, unable, because of certain character defects, to fulfill his intentions. Whether—in both cases—this represents the author's attempt to render his position less openly didactic, is difficult to decide. At all events, in the one novel where Butor abandons the procedure (*La Modification*), his hero's predicted literary career is, in the light of normal novelistic conventions, rather implausible.

Les Faux-Monnayeurs closes on a note of indefinite prolongation, with Uncle Edouard's: "I'm very anxious to get to know Caloub." In addition, it contains an apparently unmotivated murder, the death of little Boris. *Passage de Milan*, like Martin de Vere's unfinished painting, has a more real flaw, the apparently futile killing of Angèle Vertigues, which seems to embarrass both Butor and his interviewer in the *Entretiens*. Questions as to whether or not Butor actively desired it or experienced difficulty in "killing her off" obtain only confused and tortuous replies (pp. 79–87): in a way, her death was inevitable; the feeling that "there's something wrong" (p. 81), present from the very beginning of the novel, would be destroyed if something violent did not occur in the course of the night. Butor's final attempt at explanation is more interesting, however: "Perhaps her death isn't sufficiently well motivated, but that doesn't matter because her death must come in a sense from outside. From the moment she is dead, the whole of that world which is in a way my childhood is wiped out. From that moment on, one must examine that world, then leave and do something different" (p. 87). Louis Lécuyer leaves for Egypt, whereas Jean Ralon only goes in his dream, and Butor has finally exorcised his childhood. *Thematically* at least, *Passage de Milan* corresponds to Samuel Léonard's plea for an "open" future. Neither Gide nor Butor is a twentieth-century Balzac, of course, and this is the last we hear of Louis Lécuyer or Caloub. But Louis' future stay in Egypt is clearly meant to provide him with an answer to Jean Ralon's dilemma. "After that, and at the first opportunity, how could I not leave for Egypt?" wrote Butor in his envoy to *Portrait de l'artiste en jeune singe.* In making the same journey, Louis is uniquely privileged, having a chance of obtaining that perspective on our society denied to all other characters in the novel.

On a *symbolic* level, the death of Angèle, the "flaw," is perhaps insufficiently motivated but nevertheless essential: prefigured by the fresh paint tarnishing and then melting in the middle of de Vere's picture, it is in its turn a sign indicating the necessary imperfection of any book ("ruin, dilapidation leading to discovery").[16] On a *structural* level, her death is the final and most important event affecting the apparently stable organization of the "immeuble": "I took that particular night because a Parisian apartment block is a relatively stable structure . . . . I chose a relatively simple event, but one that had the advantage of disturbing the structure in such a way that all the people living in that apartment block would be brought into relation with one another on that particular day" (*Entretiens*, p. 52). The event referred to is Angèle's birthday party. But the structure is more than disturbed by her death, it is destroyed, with repercussions that are known (the flight of Louis), and unknown but imaginable: the effect on other "suitors," notably Gérard and Vincent Mogne, her parents and so on. The relationships within the building have been irrevocably altered, and the novel can continue no further.

II   *The Stylization of Language*

Perhaps the most bewildering aspect of *Passage de Milan* is the continual shifting of viewpoint and changing of style, with passages of third-person description or narration alternating with sections of reported thought, interior monologue, or conversation. Sometimes the presentation appears neutral, sometimes theatrical, even cinematographic. Moreover, the characters' thoughts are often curiously stylized, and, especially toward the novel's end, whole passages are written in a form of poetic, precious prose. It is difficult to avoid the suspicion that, quite often, the author is merely trying out certain techniques in whose place different methods of presentation would be equally valid. As Butor himself admitted to Georges Charbonnier, he was not completely in control of his mobility as narrator: consequently, the novel is "blurred" (*Entretiens*, p. 48).

While this is a serious weakness, there are many compensatory features, not least of which is the novel's humor. The description of the Mogne family dinner is a masterpiece of ironical, witty, and close observation, the nearest to an anthology piece Butor has ever produced. The undercurrents of malice and criticism, the emptiness of the conversations, the absurd ritual of precedence and plate-passing are brilliantly mocked (pp. 63–64).

The humor is edged with bitterness in the description of Angèle's birthday party; the conversation, while more pretentious and highly self-conscious, is no less devoid of any worthwhile content, while the undercurrents are more violent. At a fairly early stage of the party Félix Mogne comments mentally on his two elder brothers, Samuel Léonard's "niece," and Angèle: "Isn't that the niece of the old fool above who's dancing with big brother [Vincent]? She looks a bit panicky, wondering what he'll be up to next, very different from our inheritor [Angèle], whom he's enchanting. They've been monopolizing her, Gérard and him, since the party began, and only letting the others have the waltzes—not very generous" (p. 149). This is a relatively mild foretaste of the counterpoint of largely destructive, ironical, and jealous unspoken comments on one another by various other guests (pp. 165–79). On the surface, all is blandness; underneath, an almost Sarrautian war is being waged.

But not all the language is as crude as Félix Mogne's. Vincent compares his two sisters with Angèle: "If I were freer in my judgment, perhaps I would prefer Viola, vivacious as a maple's foliage, or the harsh calm of Martine; but it is certain that Angèle has something virginal and like a great bird about her, scarcely yet revealed, which a tiny shock could cause to break out like an avalanche" (p. 170). The jealous Louis observes her at the end of a dance: "Angèle alone is real in the midst of these skeletons clad in horrid, living rags, and she, and her shadow, are assigned to console me. May I bathe in the warmth of her mercury, her purple shadows, the tiny lakes of her eyes" (p. 193). Alexis Ralon, half asleep, thinks of Louis: "The shadow of the party's noise comes dripping down the walls . . . gnawing at my insomnia. The music alone, if only it would calm and soothe the serpent of hatred that I can feel coiling itself in his head, unknown to him, and which—I know full well—has seen its mate in mine . . . . May the light protect him . . . so that he may be spared this silence, rotted and gnawed at by a ghostly murmur which fatigue and obsession change into an inexhaustible reproach: Alexis, Alexis" (pp. 194-95).

Here, as in many other parts of the novel, it is Butor who is effecting a poetic takeover of his characters' language. In so doing, he is also criticizing the poverty of the means of expression at their disposal. Most writers formulate their characters' thoughts more coherently or poetically than a wholly realistic approach would demand, although few if any have done so with such baroque consistency as Butor in *Passage de Milan*, or produced such a contrast with the banality of other parts of the same novel. But if, like Ezra Pound, a writer finds words "deformed and diseased, their relationship a lie,"[17] why then should he confine his attempts at improvement to the "narrator's" language, when in fact he directs the entire novel? Provided one remembers that the "realism" (whatever that may mean) of Butor's novels is of relatively minor importance alongside the creation of a fictional "study for a representation," using a network of symbols and poetic language, there should be no real barrier to the acceptance of what at first must seem very strange.

There are thus two main levels of text. The first, betraying the present, decrepit state of language, comprises the greater part of the characters' conversation or thoughts and a large part of Butor's narration. The second includes the stylization of their thoughts by the author and poetic, often precious sentences or passages which stand out very noticeably from the surrounding language. They lack the cohesiveness and frequency of the very carefully planned imagery of Butor's next novel, *L'Emploi du temps*, and the author still seems to be feeling his way. But the familiar Butorian images are already beginning to appear. In the middle of the birthday party, a kind of *persona* interjects a scornful comment on human vanity:

> Learn to wait, machines forged from too fragile metal, the oil will run thicker in your arthritic joints, unable to cleanse you of sand and filings, but integrating them so well that you will scarcely feel them any more; learn to wait, things will sink into a state of comfortable myopia, the limits of the acceptable will retreat into an almost somnolent confusion; you will have your moments of daring, o weakened consciousnesses; a violet gaiety will tint your statements and steps. (p. 214)

Louis Lécuyer's nightmare ends with him sinking into sand (p. 264); his eyelids are likened to "the lips of the strait of ashes" (p.281).

After the "murder," he follows Samuel Léonard up the stairs in a kind of trance: "A pool of cold ashes has invaded the staircase. They swim in it; all their movements are as if impeded by diving-suits" (p. 268).[18] If the influence of Gaston Bachelard is suggested by this use of elemental imagery, it is virtually confirmed by Butor's treatment of "the complex of Charon" in the dreams of the Ralon brothers. Jean is carried down the Nile to the realm of judgment, to which he fails to gain admittance. Alexis has an almost Rimbaldian experience: entering a boat in a Breton port, he becomes at once passenger and craft: "And I must have lost my anchor, for I no longer feel the sea-wall's imprint, and I hear the sleeping fish rubbing along my keel" (p. 218). The boat disintegrates, and he sinks into a sea of pupils' faces, with the lips of Louis silently calling his name (p. 226). As Bachelard observes: "For certain souls, *water is the substance of despair.*"[19]

Less familiar, being confined to this novel, are a whole series of artificially lit "closeups", usually of the human body: "The cone of light only shows up the head and shoulders of the people around the shining silver on the white cloth. Charlotte Tenant's face can only just be made out, but her hands are wonderfully present, ready, attentive, adept at serving you hare, or turnips, transformed by her art into islets melting beneath a froth the color of silk stockings" (p. 55). Striking as such passages are,[20] they often appear gratuitous, and might easily be dismissed as another indication of Butor's inability to dominate his material completely. To an extent, this is true; in the *Entretiens*, he refers to the "battle" he had with language in this novel, the effort to approach his imaginary world, and hence the real world behind it, as well as the desire to retain a certain distance from the latter (p. 49).[21] But the technique of isolating parts of the body—often in motion—can cause a Surrealistic, degrading, even frightening effect. Butor's fragmentation of the human form reduces the actions portrayed to largely meaningless gestures in a framework of no less meaningless inanimate objects, where any correlation between action and surroundings has disappeared. In short, what is being attacked here is the comforting portrayal of recognizable features of everyday life, which inhibits change.[22] When the Mogne family sit down to their absurd dinner party, "Henri's whitish forehead and his tortoiseshell glasses stand out against a background of old, dark-blue velvet, beneath the dragon springing out of an old engraving, outsize claws seemingly grabbing at his ear" (p. 48). At the dance given in honor of Angèle, an arm carries a glass of sparkling wine to a mouth, where the bubbles almost cause a catastrophe: "The arm carrying the cone of pale reflections to the mouth goes slack in order to place the transparent circumference on the silver tray. The bubbles which the light wine produces in the œsophagus irritate the nasal fossae, preparing sneezes. A good upbringing stifles them" (p. 105). On these occasions, the congruence between technique and situation is absolute.

That it is not always so elsewhere, and in an over-all sense a good deal less so than in Butor's subsequent writings, may be one of the reasons why the novel is rather neglected in comparison with *L'Emploi du temps* or *La Modification*. It is uneven, and difficult to read with much enjoyment, apart from the social satire. In any case, it will clearly never attract as wide an audience as the two subsequent novels, lacking the appeal of a protagonist, the "local color" of Bleston/Manchester, or the illusion of psychology and a moral lesson in the story of Léon Delmont. Yet it marks the confluence of so many persistent and crucial themes that it cannot be ignored. In it are expressed the present crisis of Western civilization, still under the inhibiting influence of the Christian ethic and more especially the Roman Catholic church; the permanent *malaise* of all civilizations, continually undergoing change but unable to throw off the worst features in their heritage or gain advantage from the better ones; the importance of dreams; the rôle of the creative writer or artist, whose work is paradoxically the more valuable for being incomplete; the dream of a collectively written book; finally, the need for *organization*. For nothing is static: "And yet the squalid mass was constantly being stirred by eddies"; the writer's task is essentially a "putting into relation" (*Entretiens*, p. 52) of the material at this disposal, the material for a new construction, for in any case it will shift without his intervention. But his lucidity and control may produce meaningful development, above all in the key realm of language. In *Passage de Milan*, Butor has begun, although imperfectly, the process culminating in his "mobile" works.

CHAPTER 3

L'Emploi du temps

I *The Unfinished Cathedral*

L'EMPLOI du temps, first published in 1956 by Les Editions de Minuit,[1] is a lengthy book, but less strenuous reading than some of Butor's other novels. The point of view remains the same throughout, even if the complicated temporal structure makes the serious reader continually turn back—often to two or even more quite separate passages—in order to compare them with what is currently being narrated. The long, often "precious" and lyrical sentences consistently produce an incantatory, even hallucinatory effect, essential to Butor's purpose, and enabling us to fall into their rhythm without much difficulty. To those English readers who, like the present writer, have lived in one of the cities of the industrial north, be it the Manchester on which Bleston is modeled, Liverpool, Sheffield, or any of a dozen others, the novel will have a special appeal. With its unending rain, grime-caked buildings, smoke-laden air, filthy river, and restaurants which, if they are not closed, serve the same monotonous food,[2] Bleston rivals even the northern towns depicted by a John Braine or a Stan Barstow; the initial shock on arrival, the constant feeling of depression, even minor details such as the refuge in Chinese cooking (still a novelty in the 1950's), are likely to strike a chord in many readers. But the city also secretes a feeling of terror to which the protagonist, Jacques Revel, is not alone in being sensitive. Although R.-M. Albérès suggests that it would be quite possible to read the novel as if it were the product of a latter-day Balzac (not the Balzac of *La Peau de Chagrin*, one presumes),[3] anyone who tried to do so would quickly give up altogether. In the opening pages, one is plunged into the squalid world of Bleston and, at the same time, introduced to a network of images whose purpose is at first unclear: "my vision was still like unclouded water; since then, every day has cast in its pinch of ashes. . . . I was suddenly gripped by fear . . . it was just that kind of madness that I feared, that darkening of

47

my mind . . ." (pp. 10–11). It is impossible to remain "on the surface" of *L'Emploi du temps*. Like all Butor's works, it is an extremely dense compendium of many themes: an examination of the mobility of the self in time, an analysis of our spiritual bewilderment, and a demonstration of the essential rôle of literature and myth as a means of overcoming it. In short, some of the most important and constant preoccupations of its author are brought together in this extraordinary and brilliant second novel.

Revel's twelve-month stay in Bleston/Manchester is scarcely uneventful. Butor, like Robbe-Grillet, complements the major elements of the detective story with their mythical counterparts: the theme of the labyrinth, for instance, and the stories of Theseus and Œdipus. His hero's fertile imagination further complicates what experience provides, and the novel overflows with chains of events, mirror effects, and coincidences. Revel purchases a book rejoicing in the ambiguous title of *Le Meurtre de Bleston* (The Murder of Bleston); much later, and quite by chance, he meets its author, George Burton (who does not reveal his identity until later still). The encounter takes place at the Oriental Bamboo restaurant, where the book's detective first meets the victim, and which overlooks the square in which the Old Cathedral, with its stained-glass window depicting Cain murdering his brother Abel, is situated. By this time, Revel has met, through his friend James Jenkins, Ann Bailey, who in turn introduces him to her sister, Rose. When he discusses the book with the sisters, Ann tells him that the house where the murderer and his victim (two brothers) live resembles the house of a friend of their cousin Henry, Richard Tenn, whose brother was killed in a car accident shortly before the first edition of *Le Meurtre de Bleston*. Later in Butor's novel, Burton is knocked down by a black Morris sedan, but by now Revel's suspicions have shifted from Tenn to Jenkins, who had been gravely offended by Burton's scathing attack on the New Cathedral, and who has the use of his employers' black Morris.[4] This is but a minute sample of the constant interrelation of fact, fiction, and myth, rendered even more complex by Revel's account of his stay, in which the purely chronological narration of events is gradually replaced by a triple movement between present, immediate past, and more distant past.

This movement is, however, very different from the apparent

chaos prevailing in a novel by Claude Simon, for instance, where the inextricable mixture of present and remembered past is conveyed by an endless stream of language which struggles toward precision in the midst of its flow.[5] Butor's arrangement—and Revel's—manages to combine the predictability of a mathematical series with the variability produced by the impact of events and memories on the latter's mind. Georges Raillard's insistence on the regularity of the narration is not so much contradicted as complemented by Leo Spitzer's analysis of the confusion and labyrinthine nature of Revel's temporal search.[6] In common with many of Butor's later works, L'Emploi du temps organizes certain aspects of mobility (temporal, spatial, or personal) without thereby attempting to eliminate it.

On May 1, Revel begins keeping a retrospective diary of his life in Bleston during the preceding seven months. Trusting his memory, he starts by relating his arrival, his first days at Matthews and Sons, his meeting with James Jenkins and what he imagines to be the most important events of the previous October. But already there is not an exact day-to-day correspondence, since Revel hardly ever writes on a Saturday or Sunday,[7] and the events of one day in October may easily be related over a period of several days in May. In June, he continues his narration, this time of events in November, but for the first time more recent happenings are recounted and interspersed with those of seven months previously. Thus on Monday, June 2, Revel feels a pressing need to record, without delay, the details of the previous evening: "I must include all the details that will bring back yesterday evening's events when I reread this entry" (p. 83). On July 1, the events of Saturday, May 31, are related, on July 7, those of May 18 and 25, until on July 28, Thursday, May 1 (the day on which Revel begins his diary), and Saturday, May 3, are recalled. The temporal scheme becomes more involved in August (August/ August/April [in reverse] /June/ January), reaching its peak of complication in September (September/ September/ August [in reverse] /July/ March/ February). A regular progression is thus established from the simplest structure (May/ October), involving the month of narration and the month narrated, to the most complicated (the present September, the immediately past September, and four other months): the series 2, 3, 4, 5, 6.

The novel's regular progression is matched by its uniform division.

Five sections of roughly equal length, each representing a month's narration, are divided into five subsections, usually running from Monday to Friday. Each main section has a title suggesting the stages in some kind of riddle: "Entry"; "Foreboding"; "The Accident"; "The Two Sisters"; "Farewell." The grouping of significant events also follows a regular pattern: Revel first meets Rose Bailey on December 26 (p. 269) and has his first outing with the two sisters on December 29 (p. 277); he decides to write his diary on April 29 (p. 290); he learns of Rose and Lucien's engagement on July 29 (p. 276), and that of Ann and James on August 29 or 30 (p. 370).[8] Finally, as he is leaving Bleston, Revel regrets that "I haven't even the time now to note down what happened the evening of February 29, which will become ever fainter in my memory . . ." (p. 438). Within the space of approximately one hundred pages (pp. 269–370), roughly corresponding to Part IV of Butor's novel (August), most of the major events thus either take place, or are related. Only the near-fatal accident involving Burton is described a little earlier, in July (pp. 237 *et seq.*). This concentration of incidents largely explains the increasing complication of the time structure, since, as a result of what is occurring in the present, Revel comes to realize that what had seemed insignificant when first described—or not described at all because of its apparent insignificance—has assumed great importance in the light of subsequent events and must therefore be either rewritten or narrated for the first time, out of chronological order. The work's regular progression thus gains credibility and a "realistic" dimension by the careful timing of key events, whose grouping is necessitated by the effect they produce on Revel. The same combination of mathematics and verisimilitude is also responsible for the completeness of the recollection of October, since in May Revel has received no emotional shocks severe enough to interfere with the day-to-day narration of his early experiences in Bleston. January, February, and especially March[9] are barely mentioned, for the opposite reason: in August and September, Revel, deeply shaken by recent events, recalls, repeats, and sifts them on page after obsessional page in which guilt, remorse, and general despair vie with each other for priority.

But Revel's problem is not just to recapture his past. The Bleston facing him is far more than a bleak, industrial city; it is "hydra . . . octopus . . . squid" (p. 359), alive, tentacular, a personal enemy deter-

mined at all costs to destroy his mind and thwart his every move.
"Darkening," "engulfment," "numbness," "bewilderment" are but
a few of the dangers threatening this lonely and suspicious young
Frenchman. The opening pages present, in microcosm, most of the
themes of failure running through the book; oppression, loss of
direction, bewilderment, exclusion, and torpor. As he gets off the
train, Revel looks up at the "immense vault of metal and glass"
(p. 11),[10] breathes in the air "bitter, acid, laden down with coal-
dust" (p. 11); leaving the terminus, he wanders around in the night,
only to lose his way and stumble back to a different station; all the
waiting rooms are locked, apart from the third-class one, in which
"in spite of my efforts I fell asleep" (p. 15). As the weeks progress,
his situation hardly improves. His inability to find permanent lodgings
is partly due to his underestimation of the time involved, although
the purchase of a map helps a little (pp. 60–61). But if he can circumscribe Bleston visually by using the map as a guide, he is totally
unable to escape from it. One solitary attempt to reach the countryside fails, street succeeding street with unending monotony (pp. 44–
47), while his vain efforts to contact a fellow outcast, the Negro
Horace Buck, are thwarted in a manner reminiscent of both Kafka
and the Robbe-Grillet of *Dans le Labyrinthe* (p. 48).

As winter closes in, Revel's obsession with the "hostile power"
of Bleston grows so strong that he purchases a cotton handkerchief
for use as a talisman (p. 74). His feelings are shared to some extent
by Jenkins, who in a long passage describes the atmosphere of terror
pervading the town, the possibility of murder in the air (pp. 129–31);
whether this is an attempt by Butor to anticipate criticism of Revel's
behavior as pathological, is uncertain.[11] At all events, a long litany
of hatred begins to develop. For instance, Burton's book is purchased
out of vengeance, because of its ambiguous title (p. 78). Only his
hatred sustains Revel, and Bleston is blamed for everything, from
the near-fatal accident to Burton (p. 255), to his loss of Rose (p. 277),
of Ann (p. 363), and especially for his "amnesia" (p. 53), which ren-
ders it virtually impossible for him either to remember the past with
certainty or reduce the gap between it and the present.

Nevertheless, his only possible recourse is the act of writing. Revel's
diary is an act of defiance and hatred against Bleston, above all, a
possible means of self-revelation through the *organization* of all
aspects of his private life and situation which had hitherto appeared

meaningless and confusing, a personal and spatial *guide*. In mid-April, he visits the "Plaisance Gardens" (sic) in the company of Lucien Blaise, picks up an admission ticket which should have been surrendered at the exit, and burns it: "It had escaped its fellows' fate, but things have now been put right" (p. 331).[12] This "insignificant destruction" (p. 330) is, by Revel's own admission, a prefiguration of the burning of his first map of Bleston, which takes place a fortnight later, and number one in a chain of ritual incinerations, either projected or carried out, the third "victim" being the photograph of George Burton (p. 382), and the fourth, the entire diary itself (p. 378). On the last two occasions, Revel resists the temptation.

Thus, on Sunday, April 27, Revel returns home through Bleston's eternal rain and performs one of the most powerful and primitive of all rites, the burning in effigy of one's enemy (p. 296). Yet the very next day, the effigy is replaced, as his only guide (*ibid.*). Twenty-four hours later, he takes the only possible decision. The map/effigy and Burton's book, both of which are signs of hatred, but also guides (p. 114), are in this latter respect totally insufficient. If literature is at best an intermediary between man and the outside world, and one that can be highly deceptive,[13] only by my own act of writing, perhaps aided by the works of others, can I begin to organize the fragments of my life and situate myself:

> At that moment the full stupidity of Sunday's gesture came home to me—the burning of my old map, which I had had to replace.
> At that moment I decided to write in order to situate myself, cure myself, throw light on what had happened to me in this accursed city, resist its spell, awake myself from this somnolence it was instilling in me. . . . (p. 290)

The keeping of a diary is therefore the projected panacea for all Revel's troubles. If, two months after the inception of his task, his determination remains firm in the face of Bleston's ruses (this time, a succession of fine days obscuring the memory of November), his concentration is already being sapped by the overwhelming weight of the present (p. 170). The ideal project is to catch up on oneself by a constant reduction of the initial gap of seven months; with the ever-increasing intervention of the present, it may not close, but widen, become opaque.[14] With the passing of every day and the addition of every line, the hopelessness of either closing the gap, pretending that the past is immutable,[15] or even of remembering it with any degree of accuracy, becomes steadily more apparent. If the past is continually modified by the present, Revel is doomed to the fate of a literary Sisyphus; nothing he ever writes can be consigned to paper with finality, but must be constantly revised in the light of fresh information. When he leaves Bleston, his last thoughts are not of Rose or Ann, but of a gap that will forever remain, a symbol of his failure to achieve the impossible, the events of the evening of February 29.

If Revel has failed to circumscribe his past, the very attempt has largely contributed to his sentimental defeat, although, typically, the blame is thrust upon the insidious Bleston. On the purely realistic plane, his romantic ditherings are not particularly well motivated: that his initial attraction toward Ann should be replaced by a stronger one toward her prettier and more intellectual sister Rose is quite understandable, but his fear of becoming too involved with the latter sounds curiously hollow when he expresses it (pp. 168–69). Revel's own later explanations combine remorse, self-pity, and hatred toward Bleston:

> ... that Rose whom I didn't want to love, for that Rose who is forbidden, who thinks only of her Lucien, for that Rose whom I was unable to love because of this city of Bleston, because of this fight I am waging against it, this writing preoccupying me, this search that is exhausting me, in which I am absorbed, and which has taken up nearly all my evenings since the beginning of May, since I declared war on this city, since I decided to free myself. (p. 289)

The obsession with Bleston constantly blinds him to what is occurring under his very nose; certain remarks, because of the constant "décalage" in time, uncover the irony of his situation: on July 8, part of an apparently insignificant parenthesis mentions that James is visiting the Baileys more frequently (p. 288). In retrospect, the reason is obvious: his interest in Ann, whom Revel is progressively abandoning in favor of Rose. Later, when Rose is engaged, Revel attempts to recapture her sister's affection. Their evening together is disastrous, since the Oriental Bamboo, to which he had wished to take her (a good example of his obsessive concern with places and "signs") is closed because of fire. He loses his head and escorts her to a mediocre establishment where it is impossible to talk (pp. 361–65). Even a visit to the cinema is out of the question, because she has a rendezvous at three o'clock. It is of course with James, and their engagement is announced to Revel by Rose the following Saturday. When he leaves Bleston, it is, on the sentimental plane, as a broken man.

L'Emploi du temps thus appears to end on a note of total failure, a warning against sentimental dithering, uncontrolled imagination, and the error of attempting to recapture a "fixed" past chronologically. Jacques Revel, a man who combines undoubted intelligence with all the signs of a highly primitive mentality, has slid from depression into obsession; his diary is incomplete and his love life in ruins. He appears a rather pathetic and unattractive figure, and there are elements about him and his situation that recall Sartre's Antoine Roquentin in Bouville/Le Havre. We know virtually nothing of his life before he came to Bleston, and communication with his family is limited to "infrequent and trivial letters" (p. 161); his hatred of Bleston rivals Roquentin's despisal of the bourgeois "salauds" inhabiting Bouville; in his battle with the city, it is frequently described in terms of nightmare and hallucination, causing one critic to label him "schizophrenic";[16] like Roquentin, he is a highly cultured nonbeliever; he keeps a diary in order to clarify his situation. For Sartre, the world is contingent; Butor's is labyrinthine, in flux. There seems little to choose between the two.

But this analysis ignores two things: the "message," however unsatisfactory, at the end of *La Nausée*, and the allegorical poetry of *L'Emploi du temps*. Even if—as has been claimed—the last pages of Sartre's novel are ironical, they cannot be ignored, and just to treat it as a remarkably vivid account of descent into madness would be wilfully to misread it. A comparison with two of the novels of André Malraux, *La Condition humaine* and *L'Espoir*, may be of greater help. As Professor Frohock has brilliantly demonstrated, an analysis of *what happens* in these works is contradicted by their final meaning. In the first, an apparent account of defeat is negated by certain poetic scenes, notably the departure of Katow to his death, watched by his fellow prisoners, and indicating the essential nobility of man; in the second, the theme of fraternity is of far greater significance than the Communist propaganda, although it occupies a relatively tiny part of the novel.[17] If Butor's effects are more obvious, the parallel remains: Revel's very real sentimental and temporal defeat is more than compensated by the promise of a better future life (not necessarily his), thanks to the proper understanding and use of myth and literature. Revel both uses and misuses fiction and myth, but at the end of the novel, in spite of everything, he has learned certain essential lessons. *L'Emploi du temps*, as Georges Raillard has pointed out, is unashamedly didactic.[18]

The first clue to the author's real purpose in this book is furnished by his use of myth, which he sees as one of the major keys to man's true life. Butor subscribes to the Italian philosopher Vico's view that "Myths, very far from being arbitrary deformations of chance facts, recur, with a few superficial variations, throughout all civilizations. They constitute a primary and eternal sum of truths that have never been completely revealed."[19] The question is, which one shall be our guide? Revel's world is haunted by the debris of the Christian faith. He has none (p. 102) and nor, apparently, have most of the inhabitants of Bleston; the priest to whom he confesses his fading memories of the Scriptures sees himself more in the rôle of cultural guide than a saver of souls: "I have to say evensong at five, for a dozen or so faithful. . . . You will never find this nave full, even on the most important occasions, although it used to be so often when our city only numbered ten thousand souls" (p. 107).

James Joyce gave form to this crumbling world by reference to the *Odyssey*. Butor's counterpart to Joyce's Stephen Dædalus is Jacques Revel, alias Theseus, Œdipus, and Cain. His hero is well aware of the similarities between him and these Greek and biblical personages, losing no opportunity to make them explicit. In May, he takes Lucien to the City Museum and explains the tapestries to him, "while refraining from explaining to him that from now on Ariadne represented Ann Bailey for me, that Phaedra represented Rose, that I was myself Theseus . . ." (p. 253). Immediately afterward, he reflects on the similar destinies of Theseus and Œdipus, and in particular the destruction of their kingdoms by fire (p. 254). In fact, the theme of *fire* dominates the entire book, Revel being cast in the rôle of a Nervalian and Promethean Cain.[20] The focal point of the Cain symbolism is the stained-glass window in the Old Cathedral, described in Burton's book, and which Revel consequently decides to visit on November 4. At the top, Cain is depicted killing Abel, "Cain . . . in almost the same attitude as Theseus

fighting the Minotaur..." (p. 99); in other segments, Cain the
outcast and the constructor of a city is represented (p. 103). "Why
have this huge window devoted to an outcast?" asks Revel. "You
must remember that it dates from the Renaissance; the artist
honored in Cain the father of all arts ..." (*sic*, p. 105), replies the
priest showing him around. In other windows, cities destroyed by
fire, notably Sodom and Gomorrah, are shown (p. 108).

The window of Cain, Revel comes to realize at the end of his
stay, is "this major sign that has determined my whole life during
our year together, Bleston" (p. 433). But it is only part of the
astonishing network of fire images spreading throughout the novel;
among these, the destructive power of fire is most common—Revel
is an apprentice-pyromaniac, as we have seen, burning or almost
burning a succession of objects and delighting in the efforts of his
arsonist friend, Horace Buck (p. 330).[21] Any enumeration of the
mythical or biblical allusions, cross-references, and coincidences
would be endless, and various other aspects of the Theseus/Cain
myth are developed by Jean Roudaut and Georges Raillard. But
the parallels are on the whole obvious to anyone with a reasonable
knowledge of mythology and the Bible, especially as both Butor and
Revel take pains to make them so. On the literal level it could be
argued convincingly that if the latter had spent a little less time
acting out some kind of mythical or biblical rôle, his sentimental
life would have been less catastrophic. What purpose does it serve
for Revel to realize that he is the archetypal outcast and would-be
murderer?

Revel murders neither Burton nor Bleston, but what matters is
his recognition of his situation, illuminated by constant recourse
to myth, and the *example* of his desperate (and, on the realistic
plane, failed) attempt to comprehend his past by writing about
it. Butor's starting point in *L'Emploi du temps* is that we must be
aware of the complication of our situation in a runaway world
before moving on to change it. The paradox of the whole work is
that although Revel's effort is concentrated on salvaging the
past, his example points toward the *future:*

> ... all that I can do in these few days that remain is to try and complete this
> exploratory description, the basis for a future decipherment, for a future
> enlightenment, to try, as I continue, to fill in as far as possible the gaps
> in this exploratory description that I have been composing, forging, and

weaving, son of Cain, since that murder in effigy, the burning of your street plan, Bleston, since that declaration of war, since I entered your war, Belli Civitas, Bellista, Bleston. . . . (p. 387)

The basis of the future is a comprehension of the *mobility* of the past:

Thus the primary sequence of former days is only given us via a multitude of other sequences, changing, each event setting up an echo in others, ones which caused it, explain it, or correspond to it, every monument, every object, every image sending us back to other periods which we must reanimate in order to rediscover in them the lost secret of their good or evil power. . . . (p. 432)

Once Revel has accepted this fact and abandoned the belief in a "fixed" self in the past, his enterprise changes from the naïve one of keeping a "journal intime" to the mature, Proustian one of establishing a "relief map" of himself in time (p. 396). In this respect, the conversations with Burton, occupying a roughly central position in the book (one is reminded of the long discussions on the art of the novel midway in Gide's *Les Faux-Monnayeurs*), further clarify Butor's aims. Burton, Revel writes:

. . . greeted the appearance of a new dimension within the novel, explaining to us that it is not only the characters and their relationships which are transformed beneath the reader's eyes, but what he knows of these relationships and even their development, the final aspect. . . . only appearing after and through other aspects, so that the story is no longer the simple projection on a flat surface of a series of events, but the restoration of their architecture, of their space, since they appear differently according to the position that the detective or narrator occupies in relation to them . . . (*sic,* pp. 236–37)

A little later (pp. 250–51), Burton advocates the use of "reverse chronology" to obtain the same kind of relief.

Thus, while Revel/Sisyphus' task is hopeless, his example is essential. An article on Michel Leiris, written while Butor was working on *L'Emploi du temps,* stresses the need to *organize* one's past instead of just recounting it (the parallel with *Portrait de l'artiste en jeune singe* is striking): "what the book reveals to us is above all how seeing the diptych of Cranach, *Lucretia and Judith,* enabled him to transform the image of himself that he had previously created." But obviously, if Leiris succeeds in changing this image:

... the "I" of the completed task is no longer at the same stage of being as the "I" at the beginning of it, and therefore it sees the same events in a different light; it has different things to say about them. . . . The moment *L'Age d'homme* is published, insofar as it carries out the intention which brought it into being, it must be entirely recast. . . . The writer is consequently faced by a fundamentally *unfinished* task. . . . (my italics)[22]

But this is a *personal* problem. As well as being a means of self-exploration, literature for Butor has a dual rôle of denunciation and transformation of reality. One could therefore reasonably ask what are the positive results of the "exploratory description . . . for a future decipherment, for a future enlightenment." What will the future city of Bleston—or Mark Rothko's New York—be like?[23] Nowhere has Butor given us any answer, although the denunciation remains constant, and whenever the future is evoked in his work, the oracular and the Utopian are inseparably linked. In keeping with his structural Utopianism, the final symbol of progress in *L'Emploi du temps* is an architectural one, the New Cathedral. At first, Revel has no particular desire even to visit it, "because of the distrust religious art of that period provoked in me" (p. 134). Only the reading of "J. C. Hamilton's" violent attack on it as "the work of an incoherent copier" (p. 174) finally provokes an outburst in its favor:

A strange fit of blindness in a man normally so splendidly alert and lucid! For with all my newness to Bleston . . . I had been forced to admit that an astonishingly bold mind had violently deformed traditional themes, ornamentation, and details to thereby create work that is indeed imperfect, I would say almost crippled, yet pregnant with a profound, undeniable dream, with a muted seminal power, with a pathetic appeal for freer and better achievement. (p. 175)

The New Cathedral is thus a kind of architectural paradigm; its very imperfection, like that of the "unfinished" book, prepares the future, and its eventual "dilapidation leading to discovery" contains the promise of yet another building. In the same way, Revel's diary, in spite of all its imperfections (rather, because of them: its unfinished nature), will be read long after Burton's polished detective stories have returned to pulp. Burton, like Gide's Uncle Edouard, has interesting ideas about literature, but there is no sign that he puts them into practice. In spite of his friendship for the talented Burton, nowhere does Revel suggest that either the content or form of *Le Meurtre de Bleston* fulfills the kind of conditions set out above. It has served its purpose, like the stained-glass window of Cain; this in turn is replaced in importance by a vision of the *New* Catheral, whose tentacular growth is no longer a symbol of despair, like the octopus of Bleston, but a promise of expansion and replacement:

Last night, in a dream, I found myself in New Cathedral Square. . . . in the middle of an immense, terrified crowd, our eyes fixed on the Cathedral's grey spire, on its towers, on its porches, no longer motionless as befits stone edifices, but alive with a scandalous breathing, our thousands of eyes fixed on the nave, which expanded and contracted like a chest . . . on those walls that had broken adrift and were sweeping towards us like enormous waves. . . .

the walls . . . darkened . . . disappeared gradually in the fog enveloping us, the whole crowd and all the buildings in the square . . . apart from the New Cathedral whose site was occupied by a completely new building that I could not describe because I was only able to glimpse it, of which I really only saw a door, or rather only the handle and the crack, and these through the thickening fog. (pp. 405–7)

"Tilling, fratricide, construction" (p. 287): the Cainite myth has been virtually fulfilled. Revel's example, reflected by the expanding New Cathedral, indicates the fruitful incompleteness of literature. His diary will outlast Burton's books, but in its turn it will be replaced by a new, unfinished attempt at denunciation, redefinition, and change. The New Cathedral gives way to another building, as yet impossible to describe, shrouded in the mists of future time.

II   *Poetry and Preciosity*

About the same time as he was completing *L'Emploi du temps*, Butor predicted the development of the modern novel toward "a new kind of poetry, at once epic and didactic."[24] The didacticism of Butor's novel can hardly be denied; the constant relation of Revel's plight and quest to a series of universally known mythical or biblical figures, as well as the personification of Bleston as Hydra-cum-Minotaur, enrich the work with a certain epic quality. But it is also the style that elevates *L'Emploi du temps* far above the "reportage" of a year's stay in a northern English city. Butor's explanation of how to extract poetry from banality has already been discussed in Chapter 1: from strict attention to form, and especially through the use of juxtaposition, "poetry" will inevitably result.[25] In the present work, however, it is repetition rather than juxtaposition which forms not only the skeleton of what Leo Spitzer has named the Butorian "phrase-fleuve" but also provides continuity between one and the next.[26] The over-all effect of *L'Emploi du temps* is cumulative in both structure and language. In this respect, it follows the same pattern found in nearly all Butor's works: a simple beginning, related in terms teetering on the brink of banality, then increasing complication of structure allied to a progressively poetic style. In Part I, Revel's arrival is recalled in sentences and paragraphs lacking the length, obsessiveness, and complication of later sections of his diary. Just occasionally, a sentence stands out, sometimes only in retrospect.[27] With the increasing complexity of his situation—and his awareness of it— the periods grow longer, more repetitive, more obsessive (e.g., p. 194). Shortly after the announcement of Rose's engagement to Lucien, the shock of the immediate past, reflections on the present, and memories of a distant and happier past are conveyed in a series of prose stanzas, each beginning with Rose's name, celebrating her qualities, and lamenting Revel's loss (pp. 299–303). As he nears the end of his stay in Bleston, and the allegorical significance of his actions becomes clearer, the city is addressed in a series of hallucinatory passages (e.g., pp. 393 *et seq.*), in which the use of the second person singular indicates the curious relationship he finally establishes with it.

This tortuous syntax also supports an equally labyrinthine network of images and symbols. Coming from a pupil of Gaston Bachelard, it is not surprising that they can be broken down into four main families: igneous, liquid (including mud and slime), atmospheric, and ocular.[28] Their over-all rôle is quite (almost too?) clear: the opposition of sight and blindness, clarity and opacity, or the contrast of "blue sky" and "pure water" with "ooze" and "smoke," indicating Revel's failure or success in his quest, while fire generally evokes hatred (p. 332 *et seq.*) or passion (p. 123), as well as playing a supporting part in the Cain symbolism. But within its over-all significance, each family develops a polyvalence similar to that discussed by Françoise Van Rossum in her study of *La Modification*.[29] This is particularly noticeable in the case of the liquid imagery. It is nearly always raining in Bleston, a not unsurprising phenomenon in a Lancashire town; in this respect, the dismal weather is a contributory factor in the novel's surface realism. The rain also has a profoundly depressing effect on Revel, who, by the manner in which he describes it, clearly regards the weather as yet another will-destroying weapon used by the city against him: "And now, yet again, the rain has started and is beating against the panes with that gloomy, ceaseless sound that gnaws at and pares down my courage, the rain which is confusing me this evening by its irony" (p. 176).

Finally, the incessant rain, like Niagara Falls in *6 810 000 litres d'eau par seconde* or the lagoon at Venice (*Description de San Marco*) is a reminder of the passing of time and the consequent threat of forgetfulness. Amnesia, we have seen, is one of the many dangers facing Revel, whose attempts at remembering an increasingly distant past are continually blocked by all manner of obstacles, from the presence of daily problems that grow steadily more acute, to the energy-sapping cold, wet, and smoke of the city. The liquid equivalent to "smoke" is however not Bleston's rain, but "ooze," "slime"; writing in one of the more depressed passages of his diary, Revel notes that "I can salvage something of the first weekend in January on this paper strand, without taking deep soundings, without making the necessary soundings, which from now on I can only do in ever-worsening conditions, for the silt of time is thickening . . ." (pp. 325–26).

In other passages, the detailed implications of such images are rather different, although the general symbol is still one of failure. For instance, Revel's feeling of being trapped and powerless to act against the hostile city is expressed in a similar fashion. In April, before he begins writing, he is "idle . . . daily sinking deeper into the stagnant pool" (p. 331); following the engagement of Ann Bailey and James Jenkins, he feels that he is "washed, tossed, dragged along, as if in a coarse, damp blanket, by the mossy, viscous waters of that sea draining the Slee" (p. 374). Sometimes, liquid images are interwoven with others, creating a powerful but rather precious effect: "more and more sties will cover their waters' eye" (p. 166); on one occasion, all four elements are invoked: "Protect me, fine weather, or rather, since I am still engulfed in Bleston, separated, in spite of everything, in spite of all appearances and all your

caresses, separated by an immense, confused barrier from the purity
of blue sky, of water, of the divine sun, of earth and even of coal,
protect me . . ." (pp. 169–70).

A detailed examination of the rôle of the *elements* in Butor would
certainly provide the key to a fascinating "univers imaginaire," and
I have no doubts about the author's poetic inventiveness. At the
same time, the constant employment of water, fire, air, and ocular
imagery in the context of an inevitably sinuous syntax transforms
whole pages of the novel—particularly in Parts IV and V—into
precious prose-poems which run the risk of boring the reader by
their sheer repetitiveness. Many will undoubtedly be irritated by
them, and the recurrence of "flame," "eye," "air," and their
associates—in spite of their polyvalence—tends to become overwhelming rather than enriching. It seems to me that the major
weakness in Butor's use of language is its exhaustiveness, an
overindulgence in repetition and juxtaposition, to a point where,
instead of poetry, one risks having a succession of gratuitous
images or sounds. Butor claims, of course, that the poetic effectiveness of any passage must never be judged on its own, but always
be related to the totality of the work.[30] This totality depends very
heavily on the accumulation of the kind of imagery described above,
and the procedure goes a long way toward explaining his
admiration for the poetry of Victor Hugo.[31] Whether the poetic
means (exhaustiveness) are justified by the end, and whether the
reader can rightly be expected to exercise his patience to the extent
demanded on occasions by Hugo and Butor, will be discussed in
Chapter 8.

In an essay on Baudelaire's preciosity, René Bray notes that,
for the poet, "preciosity is the same in every case: it is created
by . . . the gap, more or less clearly seen, between the abstract idea
and its concrete realization," and that Baudelaire, by his constant
use of allegory, was particularly prone to write precious poetry.[32]
On the whole, M. Bray regards preciosity as a poetic asset rather
than as a fault in Baudelaire, and my own final assessment of its
function in Butor's *L'Emploi du temps* is similar. The allegorical
dimension is so obviously an integral part of Butor's novel that
to sacrifice it—and avoid the attendant risk of "bad" preciosity—
would reduce his whole enterprise to meaninglessness. "You have
lent me your mud, which I have turned into gold," wrote Baudelaire,

commenting on the squalid Paris of his time. Jacques Revel, almost echoing him in an apostrophe to Bleston, discerns "in the depths of your apparently empty gaze, the precious raw material which I can turn into gold" (p. 397). If the alchemy[33] of Butor's style has not always succeeded in effecting this transformation, *L'Emploi du temps*, by its thematic richness and provocativeness, more than compensates for its occasional stylistic tediousness, and deserves the very important place its occupies in the history of the postwar French novel.

CHAPTER 4

La Modification

I *The Process*

THE thematic richness of *L'Emploi du temps* is less overwhelmingly repeated in Butor's next novel, *La Modification*, which was brought out by the same publisher only a year later.[1] After a lengthy permutation of several time layers, both novels derive certain optimistic conclusions about the future, expressed in exalted language and emphasizing the importance of artistic creation; both make use of an extensive apparatus of mythology; their mediocre heroes fail on one level and succeed on another, the temporal and spatial overlapping with the sentimental with disastrous results: Revel's obsession with circumscribing Bleston and "fixing" his past ruins all chances of success with Ann and Rose Bailey, while Léon Delmont's obsession with Rome governs his doomed relationship with his mistress, Cécile. The greater popularity of *La Modification* is due to several factors. It is less "difficult" than *L'Emploi du temps*, in spite of the initial peculiarity of the second person plural narration and the juxtaposition of seven layers of time. The surface theme of a jaded businessman who leaves his aging wife for a lost weekend in Rome with a girlfriend, but "decides" during his journey that he has fallen in love with the city rather than with her, could be taken straight from any women's magazine, whose readers would both understand and enjoy it.[2] *La Modification* has also benefited from the French literary prize industry, being awarded the "prix Théophraste Renaudot" in 1957.[3] With Robbe-Grillet's *Les Gommes*, it is probably the widest-read and most frequently translated of the "new novels."

Although its hero is not presented to us *curriculum vitae* in hand, we do gather a fair amount of not particularly interesting information about him in the course of the novel. He runs the main Parisian office of the Italian typewriter firm, Scabelli, a thankless task not helped by a strained relationship with his wife, Henriette. After nearly twenty years of marriage, with Delmont now aged forty-five, the rift between them has almost but not quite reached the stage of total rupture. Henriette seems to despise him more than anything else, an attitude that is partly justified by his self-avowed weakness, and strengthened by her meeting with Cécile. In a brilliant scene, worthy of the psychological novel at its best, the two women are introduced by Delmont in order that they may at least establish friendly terms, thus facilitating his task when the final break comes, as Cécile unkindly points out (p. 176). The evening turns into a huge success for the two women and into a total disaster for Delmont, since the mutual esteem of Cécile and Henriette is matched only by what he imagines to be their common contempt for him, an impression reinforced by Cécile's crushing aside as she leaves: "She's much broader-minded than you, and you must stop deluding yourself—you no longer matter much as far as she's concerned" (pp. 187–88). The memory of this catastrophic *soirée* becomes one of the major factors in Delmont's subsequent "modification." His weakness and cowardice might also be described in other terms: the inhibitions caused by a religious upbringing and bourgeois life, both of which he despises in his wife (p. 177), but which he has been unable to eradicate in himself (*ibid.*). Faced with Henriette's religious fanaticism (p. 149) and Cécile's equally fanatical hatred of Roman Catholicism (pp. 60–61), he opts for a standpoint which is closer to his mistress's than his wife's, but nonetheless a result of his background.[4] "You're rotten to the core with Christianity ... even a Roman housemaid is broader-minded than you," exclaims Cécile reproachfully when he tries to take her to the Sistine Chapel. "Oh, I was expecting this to happen one day, I'm too afraid of that insidious poison which has denied me so much and is now denying me you ..." (p. 168): the "poison" of the Roman Catholic system is so strong that it results in fanaticism (Henriette), an overviolent reaction (Cécile), or a false emancipation (Léon). The "indictment of Christianity" which Georges Raillard discerns in Butor's work,[5] is particularly bitter in *La Modification*. For example, Delmont's geographical notions are unconsciously affected by the fact that Rome is still the center of the Christian world, although he would regard it primarily as the focal point of his sentimental and cultural life.

An additional humiliation is the fact that, in spite of his relatively good position, Delmont is still only a pawn in the capitalist system, as he knows full well. Why should his customers buy a Scabelli instead of a Hermes or an Olivetti, since they're all basically the same?—but it is only a "game" (p. 54), and by engaging in it he is able to indulge his wife's desires: a better flat, or better clothes for the children (pp. 147–48). Even if he is right in rejecting the false, romantic ideal of a life with Cécile in Paris, the alternative is hardly rewarding: "So I'll carry on with this false, energy-sapping work for Scabelli, because of the children, because of Henriette, because of me, I'll live at 15, Place du Panthéon; I was wrong in thinking I could escape . . ." (p. 272). As he is in this stage of mind at the end of the novel, it is difficult to regard his "decision" as anything but a weary abdication of effort.[6] It is difficult to see how his relations with his wife and children will not deteriorate further, and on the psychological level the only positive feature in his position is his awareness of its falseness.

This unprepossessing but cultured man is placed in the most uninteresting surroundings imaginable, a third-class railroad compartment, and one of the novel's many achievements is to avoid boring the reader by the mass of minute descriptive detail. Some may share Butor's fascination with rail travel, but they are denied one of its main attractions, the interesting panoramas unfolding as one gazes out of the car-window. Apart from the punctuation of the text by station names and glimpses of vehicles on adjacent roads, the surrounding countryside is all but ignored. Nothing is gratuitous, in keeping with the phenomenological outlook informing the novel. Delmont's special journey to Rome one Friday in order to tell Cécile that he has discovered a position for her in Paris, a journey toward "freedom" and "rejuvenation" (pp. 146–47), turns out to be the means of reversing his projects. During the twenty-two hours in the train, he allows the objects and people surrounding him to set in motion what is called a "machine mentale" (p. 274) which, computer-like, is supposed to provide the final solution to his problems.[7]

The process that takes place in *La Modification* appears to be an application of Butor's theory, expressed in *Répertoire II*, that "any journey in space implies a reorganization of one's temporal universe, changes in memories or in plans, in what comes to the fore, be it profound or otherwise, serious or otherwise."[8] Scarcely has Delmont left the Gare de Lyon than the process begins: "it's the mechanism, wound up by yourself, that's beginning to operate almost without your knowing it" (p. 23). The young couple facing him is one of the principal catalysts, acting as a reminder of previous journeys with Cécile and Henriette as well as a kind of screen on which to project his troubles and fears. In one ironical and pathetic passage, Delmont attempts to fix his attention "on what is there" (p. 189), in order to stop his mind wandering. Unfortunately, what is there happens to be "those two lucky people who've just eaten, their faces suffused with the wine's warmth, who are holding hands again" (*ibid.*). Almost imperceptibly, his thoughts then progress from their honeymoon to their situation ten years hence:

> In ten years' time, what'll remain of you, of this mutual understanding, of this joy . . . . Will your gaze show the same tender concern, or rather that distrust . . . from which you will be freed temporarily, for only a few days a month, the few days of a Roman dream, by a Cécile whom you will be incapable of bringing back to the place to which you are bound? (pp. 190–91)

None of his fellow travelers are immune from this sometimes feverish transference of Delmont's own problems; their slightest action can set off a train of thought. A man whom he deduces to be a law professor shows signs of anxiety, probably because his lecture is still unfinished. "He's wearing a wedding ring on his slender, restless finger," notes Delmont (p. 52), who is thereby led to wonder about the man's family, his children, whom he compares with his own, and then his financial position. Clearly, he is far worse off than you (Delmont), unable and unlikely to indulge in a similar escapade. But he is at least interested in his job, although you have a triple compensation in Cécile, sufficient money, and youthfulness of mind. Yet if you have enough money, why are you traveling third class? In spite of what Delmont calls on this occasion his "sporting spirit," which allows him to overcome triumphantly this "minor" drawback (p. 55), it becomes progressively more obvious that he detests traveling in this manner and that the inconvenience and discomfort of a third-class compartment strongly affect his state of mind.

The main object that affects Delmont is the book which he buys at the Gare de Lyon but never reads, although he handles it constantly.[9] After a leisurely and relaxing meal in the dining car, he

collects his thoughts, reproaches himself for his previous waking
nightmares—the result of hunger, fatigue, and despair—and looks
at his place, "marked by the unread book" (p. 196). But why haven't
you read it, since it might have protected you against your unpleasant ramblings of the last few hours? Why can't you open it, this
novel which has been unable to take your mind off things? Because
you wanted to be for once a totally free agent, and had you read it,
there would have been a situation in it so close to your own that it
would only have precipitated matters (pp. 197–99). This outline
of the protagonist's "reasoning" fails however to convey its
degeneration into yet another waking dream, in which memories
of the legend of the "Great Huntsman" ["Grand Veneur"] form the
substance of a nightmare equivalent to Delmont's real situation
(pp. 198–99, 202). The irony here is striking: being a cultured man,
Delmont finally faces the question of what rôle fiction should play,
even on a train journey. A common measure of the relevance of a
book is the extent to which the characters and plot mirror, or help
one to understand, one's own situation and problems. But by
refusing to read it in case this happens, Delmont merely projects
his own dilemma onto the unread pages, magnifying it in the
process, and setting his mind wandering to such an extent that,
only a few minutes later, he begins dreaming once again (p. 214
et seq.).[10]

The dreams themselves, marking the final stage in the abandonment of Delmont's project, are a splendidly contrived and completely convincing jumble. On their honeymoon, Henriette relates
to him her childish fear of the "Great Huntsman," a mythical
huntsman who would interrogate and then carry off travelers in
the forest of Fontainebleau (p. 228); the previous week, he has
read the sixth book of the Æneid (p. 83);[11] both with his wife
and Cécile, he has visited practically every site in Rome apart from
the Sistine Chapel, while a good deal of his present journey has
been spent mentally reminiscing about old itineraries or preparing
new ones; he has now become guiltily aware of the unread novel;
the customs check has recently taken place (pp. 159–60); an Italian
woman passing in the corridor reminds him of the Sibyl of Cumae
(p. 171). With the final onset of night—only the blue lamp remains
burning, like the light in a prison cell (p. 239)—Delmont is the
prey of unusually cultured, edifying, and sometimes (to us) amusing

nightmares, from a visit to the Sibyl of Cumae (pp. 214-15), to successive interviews with the Pope (p. 258), the King of Judgment (p. 259), and a line of Roman gods and goddesses (pp. 265-66). A very early dream (pp. 214-15) owes a great deal to the beginning of book six of the *Æneid*, where Æneas visits the Sibyl of Cumae and requests permission to see his father in the underworld. A later episode in the same book is taken up in the continuation of Delmont's dream (pp. 218-20), which becomes a confused transposition of Æneas' encounter with Charon, who ferries him across the Cocytus, interspersed with interpolations by the "Great Huntsman" and a railroad public-address system. The dream personage (no longer "you" but "he") then passes through a storm of shredded pages (!) to reach the gates of Rome, guarded by Janus (pp. 222-24), is interrogated on his search for the lost book, offered a she-wolf as guide (pp. 228-29), tries to justify himself before a kind of tribunal (pp. 247-48) under a bluish light, before finally meeting the succession of mythical and historical Roman figures. Although the "mechanism" is well advanced by the time Delmont begins his series of broken dreams, it is only in the last part of the novel that he progresses from serious doubts about his project to its definite abandonment. Nevertheless, their content appears more a reflection of his "decision" than a cause of it, their real purpose being to intensify the theme of interrogation, and dramatize the obsession with the "power of Rome."

Delmont's "modification" proceeds, almost imperceptibly, with the inexorability of a clock's mechanism, although occasional phrases indicate, in the manner of sudden and unexpected chimes, that the next stage has been reached. Musing on his abortive second honeymoon in Rome, he wonders whether Cécile's presence would have rendered his winter holiday more tolerable. But a complementary question occurs to him: would he have loved Cécile as much had he not spent such a miserable holiday with Henriette (pp. 149-50)? The memory of the complementary disaster, Cécile's stay in Paris a year previously, is the next stage in the alteration of his project: "if she comes to Paris, I'll lose her . . . . I must let things work themselves out. I'll see tomorrow morning when I've arrived" (p. 189) —one is irresistibly reminded of the procrastination of Constant's *Adolphe*, who is constantly fixing a time limit to the sorting out of his love affair, hoping that "circumstances" will intervene in the meantime. And of course Delmont's affairs are "worked out" for him. A momentary panic caused by the invasion of sleep is temporarily alleviated by a fairly alcoholic dinner (p. 195), which in its turn causes more somnolence. The phrase "giving up your scheme as it was originally conceived" passes almost unnoticed in the middle of a long paragraph (p. 199); five pages later, Delmont has "decided" not to tell Cécile that he has found her a position in Paris; a little later, the fatal words "that apartment you're condemned to until the end of your days because there'll be no other Cécile, because it's too late now" (p. 227) are pronounced; while the final transition is from the determination not to tell Cécile of his change in plans (p. 240) to the decision not to see her at all (p. 245).

II *Phenomenology and Myth*

You're telling yourself: if there hadn't been those people, if there hadn't been those things and those images to which my thoughts clung, thus setting up a mental machine which superimposed various parts of my temporal being. . . . if there hadn't been this combination of circumstances, this hand of cards, perhaps this gaping fissure within me might not have occurred in the course of this night, my illusions might have lasted a little longer. (p. 274)

Judged by normal criteria, Delmont appears extaordinarily passive, and the "you" voice claims that the process of "modification" is entirely deterministic:

. . . this recasting of the image of yourself and of your life which is at present occurring, implacably taking its course without your being able to stop it, this obscure metamorphosis . . . this determinism which is crushing you in the dark . . . that decision you thought was yours . . . (pp. 235–36)

It is therefore not surprising that one critic at least has stated that Delmont does not reason at all.[12] Be that as it may, Delmont's undoubted passivity in no way precludes a very close two-way relationship between him and the "things . . . images . . . people" surrounding him; affected by them, and in turn distorting their "meaning" by a projection of his own fears, memories, and desires, he is in fact an excellent illustration of the phenomenological concept of intentionality, that "compresence" of man and the world which Merleau-Ponty explains in the following terms: "The world is inseparable from the subject, a subject however which is only a project-of-the-world, and the subject is inseparable from the world, a world which it projects itself."[13] No object can exist gratuitously, irrelevantly, or even trivially, since its very presence connotes its importance for my consciousness. The self is, as it were, the catalyst provoking change, but because of the interconnection between it and the outside world, no cause-and-effect relationship is possible between "subject" and "object." "Once again, it is clear that no causal relation is conceivable between the subject and its body, its world, or its society," writes Merleau-Ponty,[14] who rejects determinism and asserts, with qualifications, man's essential liberty.[15] If this is the case, how can Butor claim in the *Répertoire II* article quoted earlier that physical movement entails "changes . . . in plans," and is the "you" voice deluding itself when it speaks of the "determinism" of Delmont's situation? The phenomenological analysis appears to contradict Butor's presentation of his hero. More puzzling still—if Delmont's actions and thoughts *are* determined by his surroundings—is his proclamation at the end of the novel of our "future freedom" (p. 274), which convinces no more than does his sudden metamorphosis into a novelist.

The first contradiction, between the phenomenologists' rejection of cause and effect in the subject-object relationship, and the continual references to determinism, is partly resolved if one accepts *La Modification* as a kind of "gageure" (gamble) in which Butor uses a weak, passive hero, but presents his passivity in phenomenological terms.[16] Delmont's own attitude toward the objects and people surrounding him would be creative of a certain imagined "determinism," since he regards them as a potential escape from decision-taking—although ironically, they constantly refer him back to his own position. On the other hand, Butor does imply clearly in the *Répertoire II* article that we are *all* affected by our surroundings and thereby denies half the subject-object relationship, whereas elsewhere he stresses the effect of our perception on reality itself.[17] That there is confusion here is undeniable, and I can see no clear way out of the *impasse* Butor has created for himself. The *Répertoire II* article does seem an overstatement, and Butor's task in *La Modification* is a peculiarly difficult one, as he clearly intends his weak hero to be, at the same time, an exemplary one.

For *La Modification* is more than a novelistic examination of the phenomenology of perception, just as the question as to whether his protagonist's decision is morally right or wrong is quite alien to Butor's purpose. Delmont's renunciation of a probably short-lived happiness with a youngish mistress for an attempt at reconciliation with his wife—at the end of the story he is determined to bring her to Rome again—will certainly displease the admirers of Stendhal. But, like Jacques Revel, the hero of *La Modification* becomes aware of certain truths at the moment when his sentimental failure is assured.

It is the realization that the historical, geographical, and above all, religious organization of the world has changed that constitutes Delmont's true "modification," reflected in the novel by the change in his attitude toward Cécile, whom he has never really loved for herself, but as a representative, the "Roman Cécile." The progress from the beginnings of his obsessive approach to Rome ("that city you dreamt about ever since your schooldays" [p. 228]) to the conclusion that "it is now certain that you only love Cécile inasmuch as she is, for you, the face of Rome . . . that you only love her because of Rome" (pp. 237–38) is carefully charted. Long before his encounter with Cécile, Rome had imposed itself as "the site of authenticity" (p. 148), a monthly refuge from family cares. Significantly, when he takes Henriette there on a kind of second honeymoon, it is as disastrous as Cécile's visit to Paris, and he realizes "the extreme fragility of this refuge which you think you have made" (*ibid.*). Presumably the fact that his address is "fifteen, Place du Panthéon" is fortuitous. Nevertheless, Delmont's obsession with Rome is carried to ridiculous lengths, and it is only at the end of the novel that he realizes that "if you wanted to bring her [Cécile] to Paris, it was because you intended, through her, to recreate Rome every day" (p. 276). On returning from Rome the previous Monday, he hangs around the Louvre looking at Italian baroque paintings and the two "Roman Frenchmen," Poussin and Claude Lorrain, lunches on spaghetti bolognese and imitation espresso coffee, and, when he finally summons up the courage to go home, gazes out of the window at the Pantheon as he listens to extracts of Monteverdi on the radio . . . (pp. 63–83).

This partly hilarious, partly tragic obsession is destroyed by Delmont's present journey. As it nears its end, even Cécile tends to be forgotten while he muses on the *myth* of Rome. Having established that Rome is his center of attraction rather than Cécile, he can now question the concept of a center itself. The first step is a simple one and does not so much contradict his attraction to the Eternal City as give it a new dimension:

> thus . . . what you should now examine at your leisure and dispassionately, is the substructure and the real volume of what you see as the myth of Rome, what is adjacent to it, what surrounds the present aspect of that immense body, as you attempt to rotate it in the context of historical space, in order to improve your knowledge of the connections between it, your actions and decisions, and those of the people around you. (p. 238)

The unthinking obsession with the myth must be replaced by a calm examination of its historical dimensions and their effect on his actions. Both continuity and change are suggested in this passage, and Butor seems to regard this combination as the essence of history, if I have correctly read *Le Génie du lieu*.[18] In the case of Rome, however, there has been one historical "fissure" (p. 274), an immense one, which Delmont has hitherto ignored:

> You countered your dissatisfaction with Paris by a secret belief in a return to the *pax romana*, to an Imperial organization of the world around a capital city that would perhaps no longer be Rome but for example Paris. . . .
>
> One of the great currents of history is thus coming to an end within you, the one in which the universe had a center which was not only the earth in the middle of Ptolemy's spheres, but Rome at the center of the earth, a center that has shifted, that tried to establish itself, after the decay of Rome, at Byzantium, then much later in Second Empire Paris, with the railroads spread over France like a black star, a shadow of the star of the Roman Ways.
>
> However strong its centuries-old hold over the European imagination, the memory of the Roman Empire is now inadequate as a paradigm on which to base the world's future pattern, which we each envisage as much vaster and quite differently arranged. (pp. 276–7)[19]

What Delmont must learn—and will only do so by writing a book— is to situate himself in the continuum of history and within a mobile geographical framework.[20] His task is to "preserve the real geographic relations of these two cities" (p. 283) and also be aware of their presence the one within the other, not as an obsession but as a *law* (p. 280). His development therefore parallels Jacques Revel's in *L'Emploi du temps*: from an understandably false, *fixed* representation of a changing situation to an acceptance of its complication. In both cases, the theme of the future, unfinished work of art is developed concurrently with the hero's evolution. Burton's detective novel, useful up to a point as a guide to Bleston, but metaphorically "closed," is contrasted with Revel's unfinished diary and the future new cathedral. Delmont's book remains literally closed throughout his journey, features in his dream as the "Blue Guide for lost souls" (p. 215), and becomes an emblem of "this future and necessary book whose shape you are holding in your hand" (p. 283). Literature as distraction (p. 203), or the fear of reading in case home truths are revealed to one (pp. 198–99), is replaced by an overwhelming necessity to write:

> I must write a book; it would be for me a means of filling the void that has opened, as I have no other way out. . . . (p. 272)
> I cannot hope to save myself on my own. All my blood, each grain of sand marking off my existence would drain away in this vain effort of self-consolidation. Therefore I have to prepare, permit—for example by means of a book—that future freedom out of our reach, enable it, in however small a way, to form, to become established. . . . (p. 274)

Delmont's notion of his book's immediate purpose and content fluctuates (or develops?) in the last few pages of *La Modification*. At first, the void to be filled is simply the few days he will spend at Rome without seeing Cécile (p. 273); a little later, he will demonstrate the rôle that Rome can play in the life of a man living in Paris (p. 277); thoughts of Cécile urge him to compose a justification for himself and glorification of his mistress (p. 279); finally, in spite of earlier thoughts on the presence of one city in another, he decides that it would be best, after all, to maintain the "true" geographical relationship of Rome and Paris, and try to reconstitute the modification he has undergone, the result of his journey (p. 283). These last-minute thoughts suggest that the future book will be essentially the one we have been reading, with its main theme the effect of physical movement on one's thought processes. But it is also very difficult to exclude Delmont's earlier aim of demonstrating how we can also be affected, when *stationary*, by our awareness of other places; to do so, one would have to ignore two essays in *Répertoire II* which make precisely this point,[21] as well as Butor's development toward the concept of mobility. Conversely, the self-justificatory argument may be regarded as no more than the final fling of

Delmont's cowardice (it is easier to justify his conduct toward Cécile in a book than face to face).

But beyond his immediate aims, there remains the long-term one of preparing our future liberty," aided by the reader. As usual, neither Butor nor his protagonist explains what this means, although one can guess. A major, implied consequence of Delmont's "modification" is that he has been able to transform his false emancipation from Roman Catholicism into a real one, thanks to his new understanding of history. If the future is "much vaster and quite differently arranged" (p. 277), our adherence to an outmoded centripetal religious system can only have disastrous consequences. What we *should* believe in (if anything) is not specified; instead, through Delmont, the author seems to be making a plea for an almost Gidian "disponibilité," through which we keep our options open, accepting and even welcoming religious contradictions as providing a wide field of choice. We must situate ourselves in relation to history, culture, and religion in terms of their—and our—potentiality for change.

However, this future freedom seems very precarious in view of the deterministic "emancipation" Delmont has undergone, whereby one form of mental environment has simply been replaced by the action of a changing physical one. Delmont's actual decision to write, necessary though it may be to Butor's purpose, also comes as a surprise. In spite of his undoubted culture and intelligence, he has shown no real signs of any vocation for literature.[22] Proust's Marcel is also about to write a book similar to the one we have just finished at the end of *Le Temps retrouvé*, but at least his creator has taken pains to endow him with literary talent. But the most astonishing feature of the last few pages of *La Modification* is Delmont's decision to bring Henriette to Rome for a third visit, in order to recapture their youth (p. 282). Presumably this is to be regarded ironically, as the last vestige of the "glamor of Rome" for whatever Delmont has learned in the course of his journey can scarcely ameliorate relations with his wife; only a few minutes previously the prospect of eternity at "fifteen Place du Panthéon" had been viewed with undisguised gloom (p. 272).

III   Time Structure

A carefully planned structure, supported by a series of leitmotives, a system of key images closely allied to that of *L'Emploi du temps* (but less dense), and a series of paragraph-stanzas indicating the hero's successive states of mind—all guarantee the poetic and thematic unity of *La Modification*.[23] The book is divided into three untitled parts, each containing three chapters, within which various layers of time are juxtaposed, according to a strict set of rules, to form a series of gradually increasing, but finally decreasing, complication (the parallel with Butor's previous novel is striking). The layers are as follows, and I borrow Jean Roudaut's alphabetical system of notation:[24]

(a) The present (Delmont's journey to Rome).

(b) The immediate past (including his visit to Rome only a week previously).

(c) Just over a year previously, when Cécile came to Paris.

(d) Two years previously, when Delmont met Cécile on the train to Rome.

(e) Three years previously, when Delmont took his wife to Rome for a holiday.

(f) The Delmonts' honeymoon in Rome, nearly twenty years previously.

(k) Thoughts of the future.

Within each layer, other times may briefly intrude,[25] but the overall division is supported by the author's own use of gaps to separate each major temporal block. One of the "rules" is that the present acts as a kind of magnet to which the protagonist's thoughts must always return after each excursion in time. The psychologically plausible movement b→c→d, etc. must be rendered as b→a→c→a→d. Each chapter contains an *odd* number of time blocks or strata; Chapters 1 to 3 are "symmetrically stable" (Roudaut, p. 138) in that there is a regular, even rhythmic recurrence of time strata within them: Chapters 4 to 6 reveal a partial symmetry; in Chapters 7 to 9, "the dissymmetries predominate" (Roudaut, p. 319).

In the present novel, the construction is both cause and effect of the "modification." Early on (Part I), the progressive introduction of extra time strata and their completely regular juxtaposition indicates the insinuation of memories and projects and, at the same time, their lack of discernible effect: at the end of Chapter 3, Léon's wandering mind has just endowed the priest in his compartment with a grotesque version of his own, so far unaltered, decision (p. 90). In Part II, the introduction of (c), the memory of Cécile's stay in Paris, is the primary disruptive factor; significantly, the less stable symmetry of Chapters 5 and 6 is organized around the complementary poles of unhappy memory—Cécile in Paris and Henriette in Rome. Level (d), the first encounter with Cécile, and Delmont's happiest memory, appears as a brief stabilizing force in Chapters 3 (once) and 4 (three times), before disappearing for good. Part III marks the virtual end of symmetry, a mathematical indication of the "destroyed organization" and the modification of Delmont's plans of a future life with Cécile. The persistence of (c) (Chapters 5 to 9, inclusive) and the disappearance of (e) after Chapter 6 are yet another indication of the change that has occurred in the protagonist, while the general progression from symmetry to dissymmetry marks above all his abandonment of a belief in a centripetal universe in favor of one governed by shifting relations between its parts. Conversely, the careful organization of even the *instability* of the structure is yet another indication of the most fundamental of all Butor's beliefs, that mobility is not the same as chaos. As Roudaut remarks: "to be aware of a problem . . . is to choose a method of classification" (p. 354).

IV   *Imagery*

In *L'Emploi du temps*, one of the principal tokens of Revel's plight was the persistence of imagery evoking torpor, oppression, and blindness. Butor's work reveals a remarkable consistency in the correlation of image and situation, and it is therefore to be expected that a novel with the same central theme—man's disorientation in the modern world—should express it in similar terms. "Ah, that threatening asphyxia! I had to flee it as soon as possible, draw in an immense breath of that air of the future," cries Delmont (p. 38), dreaming of a better future, comparing it with "this daily grind you're caught up in and which would drag you down to the stifling depths of that ocean of boredom . . ." (p. 42), or the "swamp of pitch and boredom" (p. 82). Cécile appears to him as "relaxation, smile and fire, pure water that scalds, heals . . ." (p. 208). Yet in spite of these quite frequent echoes of *L'Emploi du temps*, the baroque density of fire, water, ocular, and atmospheric imagery characterizing it has been replaced here by a less crushing use of thematic and structural devices.

The first leitmotiv, closely allied to the interrogative nature of the second person plural, is that of the "Great Huntsman," with his series of questions: "Can you hear me?"—What are you waiting for?"—"What are you?"—"Are you mad?"—"Who are you?"[26] A projection of Delmont's disorientation, he fulfills, along with the Sibyl of Cumae and other figures the dream-personage encounters, a rôle similar to Cain, Œdipus, and Theseus in the previous novel, both as external reference point and part of the book's closely knit structure. Of the questions, the second, third, and fifth are crucial, a kind of ironical reduction to the essential of the book's endless questioning and self-questioning: Delmont is expecting rejuvenation and an adventure-filled future with Cécile in Rome; he is physically in a railroad compartment, mentally everywhere else; his very personality is in doubt as he merges with Æneas to form a dream-person who is no longer addressed as "you" but as "he."[27] "Who are you?" asks the "Great Huntsman" as "he" is trying to cross a river (p. 211): this question, unanswerable in the context of Delmont's dream, is accompanied by a change of narrative from second to third person indicating, morphologically, the *rupture* in his personality.

At first sight, "fissure" (a gap already existing) and "modification" ("change not affecting the essence of what is changing" [Robert]) appear mutually exclusive. In the context of the novel, they are complementary: the final rupture with Cécile instead of Henriette is a product of the modification undergone by Delmont in the course of the preceding twenty-two hours. When the modification reaches a crisis point, that is, when the images of failure (notably Cécile's visit to Paris) outweigh those of success (a future life in Paris with her), it is indicated thematically by a series of dreams and morphologically by their initial narration as happening to a third person. For the first time in the novel, Delmont is looking at himself as it were from the outside, learning from the dream instead of himself or an external *persona*, and this "split" in his personality corresponds to the split between his original and new projects in relation to Cécile and Henriette, Rome and Paris. Elsewhere, a series of images of cracking or fissuring conveys his bewilderment. As he prepares to leave his flat on Friday morning, Henriette opens a cupboard door, reflecting in its mirror a crack in the ceiling which has been steadily spreading for months (p. 18). The fatigue already overwhelming him in his compartment almost as soon as the train leaves is likened to a high tide seeking out the tiniest fissure in a dike (p. 27); but wasn't the "rupture" of this special journey necessary and urgent (*ibid.*)? The "rift" between Delmont and Henriette (p. 37) is replaced by one between himself and Cécile (p. 245), the result of the "gaping fissure" that has occurred in him, "(a) fissure that I cannot hope to stop up, since it is linked with an immense historical fissure." (p. 274)[28]

V   *Point of View*

The final "device" used in *La Modification*, and one which has provoked more comment than any other aspect of the novel, is the use of the second person plural. In any discussion of the use of "vous" ["you"], two texts of the author are inevitably quoted. The first is part of an interview with Paul Guth:

As the subject was "becoming aware," the person concerned could not be allowed to say "I." I needed an interior monologue functioning at a deeper level than his own language, and using a form between the first and third person. This "you" allows me to describe the protagonist's situation and the way in which language is born in him.[29]

The second, published some years after the novel, forms part of a theoretical essay in *Répertoire II* on "L'Usage des pronoms personnels dans le roman,"[30] in which Butor examines successively the use of the third person and first person, and the latter's refinement into the interior monologue. But the greatest weakness of this mode, he writes, is that it ignores the *development* of a coherent language within the person concerned. How then can one put across "the dynamics of consciousness, of the onset of awareness, of the accession to language which it is impossible to account for?" (p. 65):

It is here that the second person comes in, a person who, in the novel, could be described as follows: the person to whom his own story is narrated. . . .

We are in a pedagogical situation: the person concerned isn't just someone who possesses language as his rightful, permanent property, as an innate faculty that he merely uses, but someone to whom language is given.

Consequently the person concerned must not—for one reason or another—be allowed to tell his own story, language must be denied him, that denial must be overdone, that accession forced. (pp. 66–67)

With a proper caution regarding an author's comments on his own work, critics have been sifting or ignoring these remarks ever since. A comprehensive history of the second person narrative (both singular and plural) is combined with a pertinent assessment of its rôle in *La Modification* by Bruce Morrissette,[31] who demonstrates conclusively that Butor was not the first—by a very long way—to use the second person "tu" or "vous" as a mode of narration, although in the hands of his predecessors it varied enormously in importance and purpose. Professor Morrissette also discusses the many critical interpretations of its use in Butor. Although the range is considerable, many have in common the belief that it is, in part at least, didactic, while quite a few relate it to the reader, as a kind of invitation to a similar "onset of awareness." Most accept, with differing nuances, that it is in a way "outside" the protagonist, conveying the opinions of a Faulknerian *persona* (Butor mentions Faulkner in his essay on "L'Usage des pronoms personnels dans le roman").[32] This view is supported by Butor's remarks in *Répertoire II*, which present an altogether longer and more reasoned argument than his interview, and by several passages from the novel, where Delmont appears to reply to prodding and interrogation by someone (e. g., p. 163, quoted by Morrissette, p. 14).

Given Delmont's character and situation, the explanation of "vous" as in part the voice of a *persona* does seem reasonable. The hero of *L'Emploi du temps*, groping from "numbness" and naïveté toward an incomplete but nonetheless valuable organization of his own experience, has the advantage of possessing and gradually learning how to use the main combinatory tool, his own diary. Delmont is denied everything except his surroundings and thoughts, and the alternatively mocking, hortatory, and monitory "vous" (rather than the intimate "tu") acts as a stimulation for his passivity, enabling him gradually to feel his way toward self-help and—the ending implies—the organization of *his* life in a book. But the contamination of the reader by the interrogation is much more difficult to accept. Reader identification—for this is what the argument becomes, reduced to its essentials[33]—is far too complex a matter to be equated with the deployment of a certain grammatical form. Sometimes the reader may totally withhold his sympathy or fail to become interested, in spite of a novel's so-called universal appeal, its apparent relevance to his own situation, the hero's attractiveness, or any other factors that might be invoked. In the case of the "contaminatory *vous*," it is easy to imagine several reactions: identification with the hero, partly but by no means wholly due to the use of "vous"; identification with the author as a kind of prosecuting attorney, or vacillation between author and protagonist;[34] withdrawal of sympathy for either *persona* or protagonist as a reaction against the possible attempt at involvement by the use of "vous"; most likely of all, an intellectual curiosity as to its use, reflected in the remarks of most critics.

In any case, the novel is full of qualities that are far less obtrusive than the use of the second person plural. As a fictional introduction to the phenomenology of perception, *La Modification* is a good deal less painful than the early novels of Robbe-Grillet, which in this respect are quite similar. Butor's ability to sustain our interest in the potentially dull or confusing is quite remarkable, for on this level the book is also a "gageure": Delmont observes his very ordinary surroundings, reminisces mentally, thinks of the future, has daydreams, dreams, and hallucinations. In the presentation of his protagonist's mental life, the author could have run the risk of bewildering the reader in the interests of veracity. That he does not do so is a direct consequence of his concern with organization. Each of the novel's seven temporal layers is clearly delineated by a break in the text, each stage in Delmont's "change of heart" (to borrow the title of one English translation) is dictated by the same combination of mathematics and verisimilitude as in *L'Emploi du temps*. It is the unique stylization of experience in *La Modification*, and not the novel's rather shaky didacticism, which constitutes its true success.

CHAPTER 5

Degrés

I An Exemplary Failure

*D*EGRÉS (Gallimard, 1960) may well be the least read of Butor's novels, with its forbidding appearance as discouraging as its apparently footling content. Nevertheless, it has attracted some eminent admirers, notably Jean-Paul Sartre,[1] while the author of the first monograph in English on Butor, Leon Roudiez, considers it to be a "masterpiece."[2] Personally, I disagree, for reasons which will become clear in the course of this chapter, although the book's importance is as undeniable as its thematic and formal affinities with Butor's earlier novels. There are two ways for its hero, Pierre Vernier, to escape his life of solitude and sterility: "literature or marriage" (p. 162). His failure is double, since his abortive literary project gradually alienates him from his would-be wife and ends by killing him. But his sacrifice,[3] while giving added poignancy to the eternal theme of literature versus love, also stamps *Degrés* as yet another exemplary novel in which we are meant to admire the protagonist's courage and profit from his mistakes. His obsessive concern with formal research and organization causes his downfall, although Butor hints that, tempered by imagination, it could have been his salvation. Furthermore, Vernier's almost lunatic project—to focus on a history lesson in the lycée Taine on October 12, 1954, and then broaden his field of vision to take in the "mental space" of a whole class of French students and their teachers—enables Butor to develop two crucial and closely linked themes.

The first repeats the lesson of *Passage de Milan* and, to a lesser extent, of *La Modification*, while looking forward to *Mobile*: the narrowness and bigotry of Western European civilization, blindly attached to a creed which is no longer tenable, failing to respond to challenges from within and without. Butor, and Vernier, who is a history and geography teacher, illustrate the point by selected readings from Montaigne's essay "Des Coches" in which the Spaniards' exploitation of the Incas is a foretaste of the Europeans' exploitation of the American Negro. Second, the generally enlightened views of Montaigne (*De l'Institution des enfants*) and especially Rabelais (*Pantagruel* and *Gargantua*) on education are cited in contrast to the dull routine and outdated pedagogical methods of the French *lycée* system described in *Degrés*. These shortcomings, bad enough in themselves, only exacerbate the difficulty we have in dealing with knowledge in general (p. 82)—an excellent example of the interdependence of ideas in Butor.

As the book opens, Vernier's colleague, the French, Latin, and Greek teacher, Henri Jouret, is engaged in an "explication" with his class of the famous letter of Gargantua to Pantagruel, giving him advice on the nature of his studies (pp. 10–11). As it closes, he is marking "dissertations" on "Rabelais and Montaigne on education' (p. 387). Between these two points, the reader is continually reminded of the former writer's theories on education. For their time, they constitute a remarkable denunciation of medieval educational methods, and a very enlightened alternative. Judged by modern standards, they are lacking in subtlety, far too demanding on the student's ability to digest knowledge, as opposed to his capacity to evaluate it, far too reliant on an uncritical respect for the authority of the learned.[4] In a general sense, the example of Montaigne and particularly of Rabelais provides an ironical contrast to the methods of modern French secondary education. More specifically, the weaknesses of the latter's ideal system are repeated in present-day practice. The conclusion of Gargantua's letter to Pantagruel—"In short, let me see you a veritable abyss of knowledge"—illuminates the main defect of the French *lycée* system, according to Butor, which is its inability to order the enormous mass of fragmentary information to which its products are daily exposed (p. 82).

Faced with a changing world at the time of the Renaissance, French education had to reform itself, Vernier tells his class (p. 34). In the even more rapidly changing world of the 1950's, a system that had altered little for decades found it difficult to compete with more attractive alternatives. The main battle education has always fought is within the minds of those supposed to benefit from it, and in *Degrés* it has clearly lost to magazines like *Fiction* and *Galaxie*,[5] eagerly consumed by otherwise bored *lycéens*, and mentioned at regular intervals in the novel alongside the works of literature set for study—an ironical commentary on the lack of attraction the latter possess.[6] More important still, the faceted composition of the text, in which dreary segments of lessons are juxtaposed, is a *structural* indication of the fragmentation of the knowledge transmitted. The students therefore seek refuge in stamp collecting and daydreams, as well as their magazines, to mention only a few of their "divertissements" (girls do not apparently concern them). Even their work methods betray their lack of interest: "He had the Cicero text, I had the Gaffiot dictionary. We sorted it out pretty quickly. We'd agreed that each of us would alter the style a bit in his own way, when he copied it out, so that it wouldn't be too obvious that we'd worked together" (p. 231, Pierre Eller). Michel Daval, Alain Mouron, Denis Régnier, and especially Francis Hutter all go off into long daydreams.[7] So do we all, of course, and the reasons for theirs vary; Michel Daval is concerned with an impending family move, while Hutter has recently attended his grandfather's funeral. But nearly all originate in a current or recent lesson, indicating that it has been successful in stimulating the pupil's imagination, but not in holding his attention. Hutter is sent off into a long and poetic reverie by a lesson on the slave trade, pretends to take notes, and is eventually interrupted by Vernier, who is obliged to punish him (p. 153): instead of welcoming the use of imagination within the context of a meaningful syllabus, the school system penalizes it.

One should not read criticism into every aspect of school life presented by Butor. The teachers all appear remarkably dedicated, and there are many occasions when the pupils genuinely appreciate their work. It may also be that the events of 1968 have caused the present writer to view the lycée Taine rather more critically than he would have been prepared to a year or so earlier. But just as Vernier's lesson on the discovery and conquest of America forms an unusual contrast to the "manuel"-orientated courses he and his colleagues normally teach, his qualification of the school as "this house of drudgery" (p. 241) seems a fair comment on the tedium and lack of coherence which the author's fragmentary presentation cannot fail to convey.

Vernier's key lesson does not begin with the extract from Montaigne, which will form its core. Instead, he uses a passage from Marco Polo's *Travels* to underline the impulse of *greed* behind the great explorations of the fifteenth and sixteenth centuries (p. 91).

For instance, when the Spanish explorers reached Mexico, they made no attempt to comprehend or come to terms with the flourishing civilization they found there. "Our world has found another . . ." —this phrase from the essay "Des Coches," Montaigne's eloquent attack on the Spanish rape of the New World and superb evocation of what might have been ("Why did not such a noble conquest fall to Alexander the Great or the Ancient Greeks or Romans . . .")— haunts *Degrés* like a refrain. Worse still, the economic crime committed by the discoverers of America, and never eradicated ("Whoever prized so highly commerce and trading?": another refrain) then engendered another: having conquered a good part of the new continent, the Spaniards set about importing slave labor in order to extract the mineral wealth they had discovered there.[8] Denis Régnier is fascinated by an illustration of the mines at Potosí in Bolivia, showing lines of wretched slaves, their hatred fermenting. Vernier, taking over his students' thoughts, adds that this is only the beginning of a process of vengeance which even today has not reached its peak (p. 112).

One must read *6 810 000 Litres d'eau par seconde* and especially *Mobile* for a detailed and imaginative treatment of the theme of "the black" and its effect on the American conscience, although the theme of the black outcast is already like a stain on the surface of the present novel and *L'Emploi du temps*. Horace Buck, the friendly Negro the narrator meets in Bleston, is a typical black migrant in a northern English city: badly paid when he can get work, the prey of landladies and girlfriends, he still manages to put on an air of jauntiness typical of his race. But he remains an outcast and as such appeals to Jacques Revel. The Caribbean Maurice Tangala is accepted by his classmates in *Degrés*, although the lessons on the conquest of the New World affect him very differently from them (p. 91), and it is the North African haunting the area around the school who is the counterpart of Horace Buck. With his entire face wrapped in bandage, leaving only a space for his "wolf's gaze" (p. 376), he is a symbol of exclusion[9] and a traumatic reminder that the Spaniards' crime was repeated by the French, in a different part of the world, some three hundred years later. In *Mobile*, recurrent dreams of the Negro as an enemy or an object of sexual attraction punctuate the uneasy sleep of the whites. In no case have Europeans been able to eradicate the twin feelings of guilt and inferiority in respect of the peoples they have conquered.

Butor's analysis of the European *malaise* in *Degrés* is unusual in that it is conveyed by an exceptionally lucid protagonist. Whereas Revel and particularly Delmont need the entire novel to attain some clarity of vision, Vernier, the most cerebral and detached of Butor's heroes, is able to ponder our plight and begin to implement a solution very early on. Just as Montaigne was fully aware of the narrowness of European civilization which led it to ignore the wealth of culture behind the riches it coveted, and chides it magnificently for the self-centered faith in its monopoly of inventiveness and culture,[10] in his turn, Vernier attacks "that exclusivity of civilization which it [Europe] continues to arrogate to itself, in spite of all the proofs it has itself unearthed, and which it continues to seek and produce, nourishing this contradiction, this great *fissure*, this great lie undermining it" (p. 91, my italics).

Put in the simplest terms, the remedy Butor and his mouthpiece Vernier propose is a reorganization of our terms of reference which will bring clarity into chaos, shed new light on the problems betrayed by that chaos, and thereby force us to re-examine them. Thus, the surface task of "situating" each of his students "within the school framework" (p. 89) is, on a more profound level, the means by which Vernier attempts to reduce our general uncertainty and, as he puts it, give rise to "a new awareness" (p. 82). What is needed, he realizes, is a *certain kind of projection*.

I was trying to make you understand that it is impossible to give a precise picture of the earth without distorting it, just as it is impossible to give a written transcription of reality without using a certain kind of projection, a certain network of reference-points whose shape and organization depend on what one is trying to demonstrate, and, as a corollary, on what one needs to know. (p. 56)

The one he adopts for his proposed novel is based on a series of chance triadic *relationships* between students and masters, which are exploited in a "simultanéiste" manner by variously juxtaposing extracts from classes and other scenes in the lives of his actors. In this way, Vernier/Butor kills two pedagogical birds with one stone: the method underlines the drabness and fragmentary nature of what is being taught, while at the same time it conveys a reasonably good picture of life in a *lycée*.[11]

Thus, between three and four o'clock on the afternoon of Thursday,

October 12 (Columbus Day, 1954 (as close a rearrangement of 1492 as Butor could presumably manage), Vernier conducts his special lesson on the discovery and exploration of America. The same evening, he begins writing. As he realizes from the outset, the description of *everything* connected with even an hour in a *lycée* class cannot be attempted without outside help, especially as the method (triadic relationships) turns out to be less satisfactory than he had hoped. In spite of the unusual number of family relationships in the class—Vernier and Henri Jouret are both uncles of Pierre Eller, while another master, M. Bailly, has two nephews in it, and so on—it is too much to hope that the entire body is similarly constructed. Vernier is thus obliged to invent relationships, and even antirelationships, to keep his method intact: Jean-Claude Fage, Henri Fage and M. Martin, or M. du Marnet, M. Tavera and Hubert Jourdan. He also enlists the help of a member of one of the primary triads, his nephew Pierre, who will furnish him with information.

The mathematical regularity of Vernier's method has been demonstrated by Jean Roudaut, at daunting length, and with the aid of numerous tables. As he admits that "a critique of *Degrés* would be the length of *Degrés*," I feel excused from attempting to add to his findings or repeating them in any detail.[12] In very general terms, as the novel progresses and Vernier realizes the need to "situate" the hour within an ever wider context, the number of students and teachers introduced increases along with the number of hours, days, weeks, and finally months and years involved. At its close, the "action" has spread, with enormous gaps, from October, 1952 to January, 1955, while the writing up of it has occupied Vernier from the evening of October 12, 1954, to the end of 1955. Above all, as the amount of information and knowledge encompassed grows, it becomes ever less reliable and more fragmentary. In spite of relaxing and finally abandoning the method involving *degrees*[13] of parentage, Vernier has still collected a pitifully small amount of information. By page 248, or roughly two-thirds of the way through *Degrés*, he has still only managed to write meaningfully about seven of the thirty-one students in his class, and nine teachers. Having ruined his own life, fallen out with his Muse,[14] Micheline Pavin, Vernier is last seen on his deathbed, murmuring "Who's speaking?" (p. 389).

There are several reasons for his failure and its disastrous repercussions on those around him. The first and most obvious is the sheer magnitude of the enterprise, once the implications of "an hour in a French *lycée* class" are realized. The second is really a corollary of the first, Vernier's obsessional concern with collecting the information furnished by a certain method, regardless of its value, and without using his imagination. A comparison with *Mobile* may be useful, since Butor's project in this work—the description of the "mental space" of America—appears far more ambitious than Vernier's.

Speaking of "inspiration" to Georges Charbonnier, Butor claimed that "inspiration exists from the very outset. It is present as soon as one is aware of a certain area to be explored, and at the same time of an actual material opportunity to explore it" (*Entretiens*, p. 114). Both Butor and Vernier, in *Mobile* and *Degrés*, respectively, appear to obey this mechanism, the former by his choice of America and the method of using homonyms within an alphabetical list of state names, and the latter by his choice of an hour in a *lycée* and the triadic method of description. The criterion in both works is (or should be) less the amount of information gathered than the meaningful combination of areas of knowledge by certain relations one establishes between them.[15] There is an essential difference between the enterprises, however. Notwithstanding Butor's neat explanatory formula, not only has he chosen a zone to explore and a method of exploration in *Mobile*, he has also chosen, within that zone, certain aspects to concentrate on. To attempt to sift *all* available information on America without a battalion of computers would be even more lunatic than Vernier's relatively modest effort. The content is really preselected by the normal processes of the creative imagination: Butor happened to be particularly struck by the exotic range of automobile colors and ice-cream flavors, to mention two of the more unusual components of *Mobile*. These form part of the "zone to explore" and are treated in a highly original way, but their preselection is not the result of any *method*. Moreover, there is still enormous scope for the author's imaginative treatment of any preselected theme within the context of the careful structure. In contrast, although Vernier is aware of the theoretical need to complement information by imagination, the latter is in practice sacrificed to the former: "I must get all this properly ordered, but, whatever my efforts, I know in advance that I have too few sources of information . . . . Don't you see, if I leave this compartment almost blank, it's because I have too few elements to direct my imagination one way rather than another" (p. 90). That this occurs is a measure of his desperation; like Jacques Revel clinging to a belief in the immutability of the past as the one stable element in a chaotic world, Pierre Vernier clings to facts: "this fact which is like a nail holding my text together and preventing it from dispersing, in the last analysis only exists for me, for you, for us all, because it appears as a focal-point in the midst of a whole zone of imaginings and probabilities" (p. 117). But the facts, not the imagination, end by overwhelming him, just as Revel is never quite able to dominate his past.

For time is another factor working against Vernier, who is obviously unable to regulate the flow of information he needs. As Jean Roudaut has pointed out, each "chapter" ends with a present tense—but it is a steadily falser one.[16] Even the initial "I come into the classroom, and I step up onto the platform" (p. 9) is a trick, since no action can be written down simultaneously with its performance. Occasionally, when his conscience prods him, Vernier admits his deceit: "The following Monday, yesterday according to the distorted, the increasingly distorted calendar of this account, he gave us three compositions for homework . . . . Today (but already many days ago), in the Sixth Class . . ." (pp. 276–77).

As his temporal net is spread wider, his catch is thinner, and the distance between event and narration progressively greater. And if "today" can mean anything from "a few hours ago" to "days ago," what are we to make of "yesterday" or "a week ago"? The reader's bewilderment is a sounding board for Vernier's increasing frustration and despair.

The last and most important reason for Vernier's failure is the method of collaboration he adopts. Although the terms of his pact with Pierre Eller are meant to avoid indiscretion or schoolboy espionage (p. 150), this ideal is not fulfilled, and their friendship, discipline in class, and the latter's relations with his fellow students all suffer. His classmates' suspicions that he is spying on them are at first kept to themselves (pp. 333–34), but later expressed to him openly (pp. 373–75 and 379–82). In the meantime, his uncle has been forced to punish him for a flagrant breach of discipline, but then secretly cancels the punishment (p. 378). The tension is finally broken when, after a public rebuke by Vernier, Eller exclaims:

"No, I won't go on any more!" (p. 382) and storms out of class, leaving his uncle in tears.

However, the collaboration is further complicated by Vernier's pretense that Eller is actually writing Part II of *Degrés*, giving a different viewpoint and thus enabling the "zone to explore" to be better covered. The basic idea of a second point of view is laudable, although Vernier's implementation is dishonest and almost unbalanced. What purports to be Eller writing is merely Vernier's attempt to express what his nephew might have experienced, but with hindsight as well. Not only is he replacing his real nephew by a fictional one, he is also endowing him with far greater maturity than Eller could possess at the age of fifteen. Once again, he is troubled by conscience and on one extraordinary occasion conducts a dialogue with himself, denouncing, via his fictional nephew, his dishonesty (and thereby prolonging it):

> Today, Tuesday, October 11, 1955, I am in the Senior Class, having a French lesson; our teacher, Monsieur Devalot, is making us read Saint-Simon's text on the Revocation of the Edict of Nantes,
> "without the slightest excuse and without any necessity, and the various proscriptions rather than declarations that followed it . . .";
> and I have long since ceased all collaboration in that work in which you continue, more and more deceitfully, fraudulently, to designate me by the first person. . . . (pp. 254–55)[17]

In part III, things are further complicated and are perhaps best explained by the author himself:

> In the Third Part it is the first narrator, Vernier, who makes one of his colleagues, Henri Jouret, speak, but in the course of this Third Part the first narrator gives way to his colleague who actually finishes the narrative, the story.[18]

One commentator even appears to suggest that the whole of Part III, even the narration of Vernier's death, may still be written by him.[19] Although Butor's comments render this impossible, there is no reason why we should be bound by them; conversely, the interpretation of the novel would be barely affected if the suggestion were true. Between a man's actual death, caused by a venture which is at best ill-considered and at worst lunatic, and his invention of his own death because the balance of his mind is disturbed by that enterprise, there is little to choose. His last words, "Who's speaking?" (p. 389), suggest the ambiguity of so much of the narration, and form a striking contrast to the confident "I come into the classroom" of the opening.

It is easy to condemn Vernier, yet the step of choosing his nephew and then Jouret, but only pretending to let them write, is understandable if we accept Butor's analysis of modern man's plight. His hero, acutely aware of the fragmentary nature of reality, wishes to reduce uncertainty with the aid of another viewpoint, yet fears simultaneously that the autonomy of that viewpoint may complicate things still further. Another pair of eyes may confirm what I see by complementing my angle of vision with another, or it may deny it, by virtue of being better placed. So Vernier uses another person to supply him with information, yet refuses him the chance of presenting it, in case it invalidates his own point of view. By writing up the knowledge passed on to him by his nephew, he can still control it, while he has the satisfaction of knowing that its source is external. The introduction of Eller and Jouret as pseudo-second and -third narrators constitutes a kind of magic act; the external is divested of its potentially destructive force by being controlled by the *real* narrator, while at the same time the comforting illusion is created that other, corroborative voices are speaking.[20]

In this way, Vernier's actions are psychologically plausible; he becomes deranged, but for the same good reason as Jacques Revel. A final token of his increasingly disturbed state of mind is provided by a very unlikely source, the double adultery of M. Bailly and his wife.[21] The reader might well ask himself why this sordid and banal story is related at such length. In fact, it serves a dual purpose. One of the most striking features of Part II of *Degrés* is the contrast between the rigidity of its structure and the haphazard nature of its content. To some extent, this is caused by the unreliability of Vernier's information: after all, he can only relate what he knows or is told. But the inordinate amount of space devoted to the Bailly *ménage*, instead of being used for a day-by-day account of *lycée* life, is also a reflection of Vernier's personal troubles. At a time when his relationship with Micheline Pavin is suffering because of his obsessive concentration on writing, he seizes on a parallel in the disintegrating marriage of the Baillys. As it is difficult to see how he could possibly have access to the kind of information necessary to reconstruct the painful scenes he describes, it can only be assumed that, ironically, this is one occasion on which his imagination is used. The episode ends with the rare future tense of: "The divorce has been granted, but he won't marry Claire" (p. 283), which, by its conclusiveness, may well be a prediction by Vernier of his own *rupture* with Pierre Eller and failure to marry Micheline.

As John Sturrock has observed, there is no trace of irony or humor in the presentation of Vernier's "manic" undertaking,[22] although it is doubtful whether many readers will sympathize with Butor's hero. This is due, I think, to the author's failure to convey Vernier's experience in a more concrete manner in the early stages of the book, although later on his *malaise* is presented in more immediate terms. An earlier hero, Jacques Revel, is overwhelmed by the hostile presence of his surroundings the moment he sets foot in Bleston; in other words, he *experiences* chaos, whereas Vernier *talks* about it at first, and it is left to the author to convey it initially by purely structural means. But however we react to Vernier, Butor intends *Degrés* to be exemplary; in spite of his implicit pleas for enlightened pedagogy, he still holds the old-fashioned belief that we should learn by (others') mistakes. He therefore allows his protagonists to take the correct initial step, but to follow it up wrongly. Revel's decision to keep a diary is the right one, but he cannot introduce total stability into his past by so doing. Vernier's decision to write a book, but his choice of too wide a subject, his unwillingness to allow some scope for his imagination, and ignorance of the time factor, follow the same pattern. However, his gravest and most instructive error is to realize that he requires help, but to choose the wrong kind.

Ideally, we have seen, writing should not be a solitary act; when it is, the author should welcome the intervention of the reader/critic, who, as it were, helps to complete the unfinished book. More ideally still, a collective work, a combined effort of several authors, should enable us to control and transform reality most effectively. Yet Vernier persists with his lonely, schizophrenic quest for total knowledge, pretending to use his nephew and Henri Jouret but denying them the right to their own point of view. The only chance of success would appear to come from the collaboration of all—students and teachers—since all are related, if not by family bonds, then by the more important ones of a common interest in knowledge and truth.

If all this sounds Utopian, it is the final lesson of *Degrés*. On the penultimate page of the book, Henri Jouret (the real one, not the pseudo-narrator?) sets his class a passage from Voltaire:

but his contemporaries, although they accepted the most absurd fables, did not believe the truths announced by Marco Polo. His manuscript remained for a long time in obscurity; it fell into the hands of Christopher Columbus and was of no little help in confirming him in his hopes of finding a New World that might reunite East and West. . . ." (*sic*, p. 388)

Although Columbus' hopes were endorsed geographically by the discovery of America, the "American crime" described in *Mobile* bears testimony to the blindness of Western man, who has yet to achieve the Butorian dream of syncretism implied by Voltaire's text. But Vernier's sacrifice and the "ruin" of his unfinished book are an invitation to the future reader to add a few stones to the edifice, so that one day a new—and better—consciousness may be born. Bleston's unfinished cathedral has been replaced in *Degrés* by little more than a heap of rubble, but the message remains the same:

. . . he could only erect a few bare walls, and then that conflagration occur-red which not only suspended all work, but undermined the very ground on which they stood, and that is why all that is left for me to do in face of these remains of a man's awareness and of a future music, is to shore it up a little, so that the passer-by may suffer, so that the things surrounding it, so that the state of incompleteness, of ruin, shall become unbearable for him, for in these twisted beams, this mangled scaffolding, the sun is turning the rust into gold, and the wind. . . . (*sic*, p. 385)

II   *Degrees of Boredom*

With *Degrés*, Butor's career as a novelist comes to an end, although we shall see that there is no real rupture between this work and his next major production, *Mobile*. Of the four novels, it is undoubtedly the most serious in tone, and it is certainly the most difficult to enjoy in any sense: the passage just quoted forms a rare exception to the vast wasteland of the text. One looks in vain for some echo of the baroque imagery of *L'Emploi du temps*, the Surrealistic effects of parts of *Passage de Milan*, or the leitmotives of *La Modification*. The novel does possess a certain rhythm set up by the regular structure; phrases of Rabelais and Montaigne, and titles of books, especially school manuals, do recur, but with insufficient frequency to create any poetic effect. Professor St. Aubyn sees a strong resemblance between the "faceted" construction of *Degrés* and "the series of unexpected and opposing figures of speech found in Surrealist poetry."[23] But there is an enormous gap between the drab "simultanéisme" of:

> Uncle Henri came down from the first floor. . . .
> Denis Régnier had come back from his father's in tears. . . .
> M. Hubert was taking his pregnant wife for a gentle walk. . . .
> M. Moreux helped us load the trunks on his van. . . . (p. 163)

and the vital, intriguing and amusing:

> The government had just fallen
> Into a hawthorn bush
> A general strike of strand stretched for as far as one could see
> Under the combined influence of the moon and headache.
>   (Louis Aragon, "Mimosas")

Degrés poses the problem which was first raised in French literature with the publication of Flaubert's *L'Education senti-mentale*: how to present the inherently dull or boring. But whereas a close reading of Flaubert's masterpiece permits great enjoyment to be obtained from the stylistic delicacy and constant irony which transform dullness into poetry, Butor deliberately denies himself the use of such instruments. Vernier presents his information in the way he does in order to convey the dreariness of school life, the dull, compartmented transmission of knowledge in the classes, and thereby to bring about "a new awareness." But I believe it was mistaken to allow him to go so far in this respect, when the kind of stylistic counterpoint adopted, although haphazardly, in *Passage de Milan*, would have permitted the necessary condemnation of a certain kind of reality and the language describing it, while relieving the monotony. Butor is in danger of losing the interest of even the most dedicated and perspicacious among his readers and, as John Sturrock has suggested, of persuading the less acute that there is really nothing there at all.[24] Significantly, the most enthusiastic critics of *Degrés* are not only Sartre and Roudiez, but people like Jean Ricardou, who descend to even murkier depths of unreadability in their own "novels." While it is thematically important, *Degrés* does not exemplify the intellectual/poetic balance Butor is always seeking, and which is brilliantly achieved in his next major work, *Mobile*.

CHAPTER 6

Mobile

I *The Principle of Mobility*

PRESENT-DAY North America clearly fascinates the peripatetic Butor. Since 1960, he has visited the United States on numerous occasions, mainly as a visiting professor teaching in various universities; for example, in 1969–70 he spent a large part of the American academic year at the University of New Mexico. That his visits should have stimulated Butor to write about America is really no more surprising than the determination that *his* travel book should not conform to the accepted pattern. When *Mobile* was published by Gallimard in 1962, the "orgy of surprises and thrills" ironically announced on the back cover proved too much for critics accustomed to traditional travel fare, among whom Pierre-Henri Simon (*Le Monde,* March 7) elegantly accused Butor and his readers of collective insanity, while Kléber Haedens headed his account in *Candide* (March 22): "The true motive ["mobile"] of Michel Butor or the extent of credulity and stupidity in 1962."

Butor is not insane of course; *Mobile* remains one of the peaks of his achievement and is the first of a series of "mobile" works whose form is dictated by their purpose. That the post-1962 creative works *look* so different from the four novels does not indicate a rupture in the continuity of Butor's production but rather a culmination of tendencies already present long before *Mobile*. Even if he has apparently abandoned prose fiction as a medium, his treatment of it was in any case so unconventional that to compare the "novel" *Degrés* with the poem(?) *Mobile* would be to beg the question of literary genres.

One of the most distinctive characteristics of Butor's novels is their protagonists' inability to cope adequately with the information assailing them, a weakness they share with Robbe-Grillet's narrators. The consequences are interesting: although one of the mainstays of prose fiction has always been some sort of central consciousness, in his very first novel Butor chose to replace the focal point of view by a wandering author's consciousness, invading the minds of various characters in turn. Although the next novel is narrated by a protagonist—whose main characteristic is bewilderment—the hero of *La Modification* is continually addressed by a *persona*, and the "real" narrator of *Degrés* pretends to employ two others, one of whom ironically does take over at the end. The individual's efforts may be exemplary, but are nonetheless insufficient; having experimented with this pattern in three novels, Butor decided to replace the fictional consciousness by his own and to entitle the product quite unambiguously: "*Mobile*, study for a representation."[1] The reader is thus left in no doubt as to the provisional nature of Butor's text, while its disjointed form demands his collaboration: *Mobile* is much more than a compendium of Butor's impressions of America; through it, the author wishes to join with us in a collective examination of America which, he hopes, will point the way to change: in this sense, it is a very humble work. The "quilt" form of *Mobile* is neither symmetrical nor pretends to be definitive; Butor, the enemy of the "closed" or "finished" book, takes *his* lesson from a counterpane in the Shelburne museum, whose designer has attempted to ward off evil by destroying the symmetry of his pattern: "the gods alone can create perfection and . . . mankind would be presumptuous to try and produce flawless works" (*Mobile*, p. 181). And if an author—whom one expects to be a man of unusual perceptiveness and sensitivity—is so aware of his own limitations, we ought not to be shocked by his characteristically geometric relegation of the individual in general: "Imagine circles and their points of intersection. The final limit is the moment at which we apprehend the individual in what might be called his absolute difference."[2]

The individual's "decentralization" is accompanied in *Mobile* by a complete renunciation of linear construction. Once again the process is one of experimentation with elements already present in the earlier works, and not a sudden break with established techniques, since all four novels combine a linear framework with discontinuous narration in one form or another. Even in *Passage de Milan*, the main narrative line (7:00 P.M.–7:00 A.M.) encloses sections of text which represent simultaneous rather than successive viewpoints, a method which is taken up again in *Degrés*. The two other novels present, respectively, a to-and-fro movement between present, immediate past, and more distant past (*L'Emploi du temps*), and between several pasts, the present, and the future (*La Modification*). *Mobile* abandons all pretense at progressive narration in time: its contents are present simultaneously, permitting a variety of reading itineraries, or simple flicking through.[3] However, this does not imply that there is no historical dimension *within* the book or that parts of it cannot be read in the normal manner, one page succeeding another; Butor has succeeded in achieving thematic progression without the progression in fictional or historical time normally accompanying it. Above all, he is anxious not to impose on his readers a rigid, successive arrangement (however provisional) of a reality which he recognizes as mobile, or, to use Roland Barthes's term, "discontinuous."[4] The essence of American "reality" consists for Butor in the ever shifting relations between a historical dimension, an unconscious one which owes something to Jung's theory of archetypes in its collective nature, a conscious one which is again collective rather than individual, and an "objective" one, formed by the objects of the collective consciousness. A mobile presentation of these elements is attempted by imposing an order which is at once neutral and cannot help but be subjective, but which still allows the maximum amount of freedom to the reader. To what extent this is actually achieved will soon become clear.

After its appearance and discontinuity, the final surprising feature of *Mobile* is the amount of secondary material (catalogues, prospectuses, quotations by famous historical figures, etc.) incorporated in the text. Yet again, this is only an extension of a technique already used in *Degrés*, which contains a respectable proportion of the same kind of material: quotations from Rabelais, Montaigne, and other authors, or enumerations of school textbooks. The wholesale pillaging of secondary material characteristic of *Mobile* and later poetic works, notably *Illustrations*, reflects Butor's refusal to honor the sacrosanct, "closed" book, and his concept of the chain of works, both "critical" and "creative," which continue and complement what has gone before.[5] No writer is a closed domain; his works must be reread, "piously profaned," as Butor puts it in his essay on Hugo's novels.[6] If the profanation involves the inclusion of extracts from other authors in one's own text, respect rather than disrespect is normally intended.[7] The concept of collaboration between author and reader is thus extended to encompass a kind of retrospective, or even "posthumous" collaboration between one author and another. Finally, the inclusion of secondary material is yet another reminder of our separation from reality by the wall of information, true, half true, and false, which surrounds us on every side. Encyclopedias, catalogues, dictionaries, and the like have an equally privileged place alongside the texts of great authors, according to Butor:

> . . . to create a novel, one must remain in the realm of the everyday story, it has to be something that somebody might have told somebody else. But it is possible to treat printed works in a manner similar to the novel when it uses these everyday stories: works like dictionaries, encyclopedias, catalogues, calendars, directories, guides, manuals, which are made up of elements common to innumerable possible stories, which are like the knots in the fabric of information surrounding us and through which we view reality.[8]

The solution to the problem of how to set out a "mobile" work lacking a central narrative consciousness or a progressive story, but crammed with heterogeneous primary and secondary material, can be found in several theoretical texts, extending over quite a long period, and all concerned wholly or partly with the physical properties of the "book-as-object." The most important appeared a few months after the publication of *Mobile*; entitled "Le Livre comme objet," it cites authors as diverse as Rabelais and Mallarmé who, in their various ways, have experimented with the disposition of print on the page. Butor claims that the book possesses an innate advantage over the far more recent inventions of motion picture, record player, or tape recorder: reader mobility; we can turn back or forward in a book far more easily than we can wind back a tape recorder or return to a given point in a record, while the motion picture offers us virtually no such possibility, since, like the gramophone or tape recorder, it is essentially a *successive* medium. Exploitation of this advantage by use of different kinds of type, disposition of print anywhere within the limits of the page, and introduction of blank spaces and margins to separate the text horizontally and vertically, provides even greater mobility for the reader as well as allowing great scope for Butor's main poetic device of juxtaposition: parts of the text can affect others by virtue of their contiguity.[9]

II *Structure and themes*

In spite of its title, *Mobile* is not dedicated to Alexander Calder,[10] but to the American painter Jackson Pollock,[11] whose action paintings complement emotion and spontaneity with a higher degree of conscious ordering than is often admitted: *controlled* chance is responsible for the final result, not the completely random dripping of paint on canvas which Pollock is widely but erroneously thought to have practiced. In the same way, the apparently haphazard distribution of the components of *Mobile* conceals a framework which is planned with extreme care, yet still permits the reader wide discretion in his choice of itinerary. The book's basic structure is that of an onomasticon: within an alphabetical list of the states forming its fifty sections, established according to their French names (e.g., "Caroline du Sud" and not "South Carolina"), a second list of the most frequent town homonyms is used to create "resonances" within states adjacent physically or alphabetically—for instance, the town of Corning (Arkansas) has homonyms in Missouri and the next state further north, Iowa, as well as the next state alphabetically, California.[12] Alphabetical order and geographical proximity are thus the two governing factors, and both may appear random or neutral. In a way, they are, but their random nature is paradoxically calculated to produce a definite effect.

Roland Barthes has argued in his highly perceptive essay on *Mobile* that the alphabetical list recalls the arbitrary, federal nature of America and creates a poetic contiguity.[13] There is also another important consequence of the book's order—the feeling of decentralization created by a plan which takes the reader from the Atlantic to the Pacific and may than deposit him on the frontier of Mexico. The United States, unlike France—and this is a fact which would particularly strike a Frenchman—is not a country whose culture and population are siphoned off by one center; San Francisco, Chicago, California, or Texas are of far more importance in relation to New York City or State than Marseille or Lyon are to the Parisian region. New York therefore waits its turn in *Mobile* after Chicago, Los Angeles, and a score of important cities and states, and the reader's haphazard journey from state to state, involving a continual criss-crossing of America, is echoed by the important theme of travel, represented by the "snapshots" of cars in the country, generally going faster than the speed limit allows, and clearly heading for a very distant goal. As they do so, they pass through a succession of towns which may well bear identical names—a kind of onomastic by-product of the American mass-production mentality. Butor divides the place names into four categories: European, famous American, Utopian, and Indian (*Entretiens*, pp. 159–60); and he is even willing to forego his principle of frequency for thematic reasons: it is unlikely that statistics are responsible for the number of nostalgic localities at the beginning of *Mobile* (Cordova, Florence, La Grange) or the Utopian and natural ones at its end (Eden, Buffalo, Elkhorn).

Each place name is linked to a "cell" with a core in italics and an outer shell in roman, to use Butor's own terminology (*Entretiens*, p. 157). The shell tends to be prosaic and factual, including, among other things, geographical information, details of local flora and fauna, or extracts from advertisements and catalogues. The core contains some secondary material, such as quotations from the writings of famous Americans, but also includes poetic presentations of the sea, fish, birds, and vegetation, as well as urban poems formed from details of restaurants, foreign-language radio programs, and so on. All the material relating to the "primary" state (formed of several cells) starts at the extreme left-hand margin, whereas that belonging to adjacent states is indented:[14] an important feature of *Mobile* is the "presence" within each state of material relating to other, contiguous ones, which may almost overwhelm it. Vermont, one of the tiniest states, is thus dominated by Massachusetts and New York, and the section on it is one of the longest in the book.

The structural time-span of *Mobile* is approximately forty-eight hours, in the course of which all fifty states are visited, some much more briefly than others, and many at night. The proportion of primary and secondary material also varies considerably from state to state, depending on many factors, including position in the alphabet, proximity to other states or the sea, or the presence of a historical dimension. Occasionally, the scheme is abandoned altogether: Washington is visited at night, but the center of the national consciousness can hardly be ignored by Butor, who composes a fantasy guide to the "sacred city of Washington" (p. 131) on the lines of a thirtieth-century *Blue Guide*; the greater part of the section on the state of Oregon is occupied by the three juxtaposed prospectuses of Clifton's Cafeteria (California). But in general the only real variation is provided by the greater or lesser emphasis on italicized or roman material and by the reappearance of certain obsessional themes which can be followed at the reader's discretion.

For in spite of the effects of humor and incongruity produced by the juxtaposition of unexpected elements, *Mobile* presents a somber picture of American history and present-day society—so somber that it is at first difficult to understand the author's obviously genuine liking for a country he has visited so often. Founded on a series of murders[15] perpetuated in the national consciousness by the whites' guilt and the blacks' hatred, the home of conformism and inequality, Butor's America seethes with a violence which was barely suppressed in 1960 but had begun to erupt a few years later. In an effort to control it, American society romanticizes its history through therapeutic institutions like "Freedomland," where the public is given an opportunity to relive a cellophane-wrapped past of spectacular fires, Civil War adventures, and battles against Indians—or through visits to carefully selected, picturesque reservations.

One of the very real merits of *Mobile* as a social document is to draw attention to the history and plight of the American Indian by a variety of sometimes subtle, sometimes quite brutal means. Butor adopts Chateaubriand's view of the pre-Columbian Indian as a symbol, not of Rousseauesque primitiveness, but of a more ancient and less contradictory way of life than ours; America's isolation had saved it from the perpetual war between the Christian and Antique traditions which splits the European consciousness.[16] When the European settlers first arrived, they found a civilization far older than their own, as Butor reminds us at the very beginning of *Mobile*: "The Ocmulgi tumuli show traces of six successive civilizations, the most ancient probably dating back to 8000 B.C., the most recent dying out in the eighteenth century . . ." (*sic*, p. 17). The simplest answer to the challenge of a different and thriving culture was adopted, and the Indians were exterminated or deported:

The most powerful tribes of North Florida were the Appalachians and the Timucua; the latter, numbering thirteen thousand in 1650, were wiped out in less than a century by warfare and disease. A few survivors were possibly deported to Oklahoma, at that time designated as Indian territory, with a number of Seminoles. Others emigrated to Cuba in 1763. . . . (sic, p. 36)

Those still remaining were converted, with curious results, particularly in the nineteenth century, when numerous native visionaries combined the teachings of Christ with the "religion" of Peyotl (mescalin) to attract large numbers of followers. Butor's source, Vittorio Laternani, is quoted at length on some of the more extraordinary cases, in which the white man himself was occasionally contaminated.[17] The story of the Indian Sequoyah is rather different; he absorbed the white men's knowledge so well that he invented an alphabet in order that his people's language could be translated, thereby incurring the suspicion of his teachers, who burned down his house as a protection against witchcraft (pp. 18–19).

In Butor's day, such barbarity has been replaced by the subtler oppression of using the Indians as tourist-fodder. One of the chief attractions of rural Michigan is a slice of authentic American history (to lapse into publicity jargon):

". . . Indian Ceremonials . . ."
"On beautiful lake La Chapelle, a short distance from National Highway 23 and Highway 55 to Michigan, 9 miles west of East Tawas and Tawas city, by a good forest road
—the famous old timber road,
—genuine North American Indians will demonstrate their ceremonies for your pleasure! The open air arena, comfortable and picturesque, looks onto a wooded island used as a stage. Open air snack bar and large, well-lit parking area. . . ." (sic, p. 84)

For the most part, however, the Indians are neither actively suppressed nor exploited, but just forgotten or deliberately ignored, languishing on the innumerable reserves dotting America. "Reservation of the [X] Indians" rapidly becomes ". . . of the [X] Indians", or even "—. . . of lake Nett" (sic, p. 31), indicating the indifference (or repression of an uncomfortable reminder?) on the part of the hasty traveler who tears past in his pear-colored Nash or pistachio Dodge.

The Indian, "expression, countenance, language of this scandalous continent" (p. 107), inspired too much terror to be domesticated by the white man, who consequently imported slave labor from Africa. This time, however, the attempt at mental repression has been less successful. "For whites only" may well be supplanted by "whites only" and then "only" (all in English in Butor's text), echoing the "—of the [X] Indians," but, awake or asleep, white man is haunted by fear and hatred of his black neighbors. In early sections of *Mobile*, the Negro's presence is insinuated by the never-ending references to the color bar, while with the onset of night it is felt in a series of nightmares of frightening intensity (e.g., p. 149). In the southern states of Oklahoma (pp. 219–28) and Tennessee (pp. 264–86) the white man's litany of terror, sexual jealousy, and hatred reaches its climax, with the justificatory measure of segregation finally proposed:

Blacks they creep along our walls (. . . .) Blacks they look at our shopwindows (. . . .) Blacks they hang around our streets (. . . .) Blacks they undress our daughters with one nostalgic look (. . . .) You say we hate them, but look at them! Can't you see they're invading us and that they won't forgive us? [pp. 219–27]. *Thus, in spite of these barriers, we are daily losing ground before this immense menace, and if we're covering ourselves with opprobrium, at least it obliges our governments to stiffen the segregation laws protecting us. . . . (sic, p. 269)*

Thomas Jefferson's arguments are much subtler, and carefully selected extracts from them are placed in the sections of *Mobile* dealing with Georgia, Kentucky, Tennessee, and his own state (then colony) of Virginia.[18] Jefferson is best known as the main drafter of the American Declaration of Independence and one of the earliest and most vigorous champions of the Negro, fighting for the abolition of slavery, although Butor's selections from the *Notes on the State of Virginia* create a very different impression. Prefaced ironically by the key phrase of the Declaration of Independence— "We hold these truths to be self-evident, that all men are created equal . . ." (p. 41)— they emphasize Jefferson's profound belief in the *inequality* of races, resulting from the "real distinctions which nature has made" (p. 43). His arguments are based on intellectual, moral, and esthetic grounds: the blacks are inferior in reasoning power, and their imagination is poor; they lack prudence, and for them love is more an animal passion than "a tender delicate mixture of sentiment and sensation" (p. 123); they are less handsome than the whites, incapable of creating beauty, and their real musical ability is in doubt. Having concluded his analysis, Jefferson appears almost frightened by what he has written, replacing his assertion of the Negro's intellectual inferiority by a "suspicion" that this may be so, and speaking of the "unfortunate" difference in color.[19] But the text remains a frightening document of racialism, the more so by the sophisticated moderation of the thesis. The only point at issue is to what extent the "true" Jefferson is revealed. Dos Passos and the editor of the modern edition of the *Notes*, William Peden, seek to redress the balance by reference to his personal dealings with Negroes, both quoting a letter to a Negro mathematician and surveyor, Benjamin Banneker, in which he writes of his wish "to see such proofs as you exhibit, that nature has given to our black brethren, talents equal to those of the other colors of man, and that the appearance of a want of them is owing merely to the degraded condition of their existence. . . . "[20] There is also evidence that Jefferson treated his own slaves most liberally, probably in the patriarchal manner implied by the tone of a letter to some Indian chiefs cited in *Mobile* (p. 315), in which they are addressed as "My children." Moreover, as Peden remarks (p. 286), his written views must be placed in their historical and geographical context, where they appear "startlingly advanced." But if Butor is unfair to Jefferson, the use of the *Notes* is plainly justified on polemical grounds. Racialism is not a prerogative of the ignorant; it has never lacked in skilled theoricians, whose sometimes well-meaning writings have been adopted by madmen or bigots. And by examining its progress in America, Butor is in any case doing no more than holding up a mirror to our own society in Western Europe: the prosperity of Nantes is built on the slave trade (*Entretiens*, p. 231).

The second great apostle of inequality presented in *Mobile* is Andrew Carnegie, whose *The Gospel of Wealth* marks the final stage in the deterioration of the principle of fraternity which had governed the very early settlers' dealings with the Indians. For the seventeenth-century Quaker William Penn, goodwill on the part of the white man and the Indian would solve any differences between them, as Butor's quotation of his treaty with the Delaware tribe indicates (pp. 73–74). In the eighteenth century Benjamin Franklin's

Information to Those who would Remove to America, serialized by
Butor to form a bridge between Penn and Carnegie, the accent has
shifted from goodwill to the attractions of America for settlers
willing to work for their fortunes: "Who then are the kind of persons
to whom an emigration to America may be advantageous? And
what are the advantages they may reasonably expect . . ." (*sic,* p. 246);
a nation's morality is guaranteed by industriousness and full
employment (p. 317). . . . For the nineteenth century Carnegie, the
archetypal self-made man who profited from hard work (and that
of his employees), the law of capitalism is hard for both workers
and masters but ensures the survival of the fittest in all areas.
"At the end of his life, Andrew Carnegie sold his steelworks at
Pittsburgh to John Pierpont Morgan and devoted himself to good
works," the text laconically reports (p. 250), leaving the reader to
supply the reason for the multimillionaire's tardy philanthropism.
Butor's reason is stated quite unequivocally to Georges Charbonnier: guilt and despair.[21] What is perhaps worst in Carnegie's text—
and this is not brought out in Butor's quotations—is his justification
of the "gospel" by reference to the Bible and a sermon of John
Wesley, both of which, he claims, amply justify the accumulation of
wealth.[22] But elsewhere in *Mobile,* the publicity for Clifton's
cafeteria provides a more up-to-date illustration of the alliance
between business and religion—for the profit of the former rather
than the latter (pp. 234–42).

"The hard sell": if Butor's interpretation of American history is
largely governed by his dislike of inequality and exploitation, his
picture of mid-twentieth-century America emphasizes, structurally
and thematically, the principles of mass production and consumer
wooing. *Mobile* itself is remarkably like a catalogue: it can be
opened at random, or selectively, and overwhelms at first by the
variety of its contents and their diverse presentation, with the italicized
sections performing roughly the same function as illustrations.
Within it, catalogues and prospectuses abound. Clifton's cafeteria
employs insinuation, playing on the public's curiosity in order to
stimulate custom, whereas the mail-order catalogues of Sears
Roebuck and Montgomery Ward invite one to purchase by the
almost unbelievable range of goods offered and, within that range,
variations on the same ware; the principle of "custom-made"
clearly no longer applies just to automobiles in the United States

but has spread to nearly all manufactured goods, from antiage preparations (pp. 88–91) to nylon knickers (pp. 174–75). At the other extreme, the Coca-Cola or Heinz signs winking at night, or the "Freedomland" brochure, provide a cruder invitation to buy or sample. In this assault of choice, *colors* play a vital rôle, particularly where automobiles are concerned. First described by make alone, then by simple colors—gray, blue, red, yellow, etc.—they are then distinguished synæsthetically, in terms of taste and smell; the "enormous old mirabelle-colored truck" passing the "plum-colored Nash" (p. 194) or the "mango-colored Studebaker" passing a stationary, strawberry-colored one (p. 273), set up a grotesque echo of the ice-cream flavors available at any Howard Johnson restaurant, and which are enumerated throughout *Mobile*. It is not enough for our visual sense to be stimulated, but an attack is also made on our taste buds.[23]

Almost every page of *Mobile* abounds in a near-superfluity of objects, many of which are literally consumed: gasoline (B.P., Esso, Caltex, etc.), ice creams, in all their sickly attractiveness (apricot, almond, black-currant, plum, mirabelle, etc.), special food (Cantonese, Dutch, Creole, Turkish, Indonesian, etc.), drink (Coke, Pepsi), tobacco (Chesterfield, Lucky Strike), and so on. But where is the consumer? Disembodied voices greet one another ("Hello, Jack"), speak on telephones, or look at their gas gauges ("we must fill up at the next Caltex"); other anonymous people combine in a chant of hatred against the blacks. But no contemporary American of any distinction speaks or writes, apart from Governor Rockefeller pronouncing a benediction on "Freedomland" (the law of libel may be partially responsible for this). One knows that Butor is not interested in the individual, since what concerns him is the American consciousness in general. Even so, modern American man—even in his disembodied form—has little to say in *Mobile*. His *presence* is felt on practically every page, but it is insignificant alongside the surrounding objects. Leered down on from billboards by the illuminated faces of the new gods (film stars), assailed by advertisements, brochures, and catalogues, frantically consuming Howard Johnson ice creams, Cantonese food and B.P., he is the ultimate victim of the society created by his ancestors' greed. The weight of objects in *Mobile* is crushing; alongside—or beneath—them, the individual is reduced to a degree of insignificance even greater than that implied by Butor's theories. Of all his works, *Mobile* is the only one to which Lucien Goldmann's Marxist analyses of the "autonomous universe of objects, with its own structure and its own laws, and through which alone human reality can still express itself to some extent," may with justification be applied.[24]

If man has almost lost the battle against objects, there remains the presence of nature. Butor combines a fascination with the developments of American civilization, notably the material or artificial side, with a nostalgia for the unspoiled continent of Chateaubriand's day, which is revealed in a variety of ways. Alongside the enumerations of automobiles, ice-cream flavors and the like, descriptions of John James Audubon's famous bird illustrations provide a natural (and ironical?) counterpart to the repetition-cum-modification of the modern American economy, and italicized prose-poems on the theme of the sea act as an accompaniment to many sections. Often the sea poems are interwoven with others presenting fish, birds, precious stones, fruits, flowers, and plants in a kind of poetic celebration of nature (e.g., Florida, pp. 35–38). On their own, they have a variable function, indicating the spread of sophistication (p. 28), symbolizing purification and cure (p. 177). Sometimes, the sea poems also function as a comment on or reaction to contiguous themes; in New York and neighboring states the sea is contaminated by urban life, whereas in Maine, the most distant of the chain of states within the New York section, it regains its purity (pp. 197–208); in the southern states, it forms a background to the seduction patter of an anonymous Negro who, under the protection of night, has taken his white victim to a deserted beach (pp. 275–91); it is called upon as a symbol of purification during the account of the trial of the witches of Salem (pp. 170–77).

But it is the over-all presence of the sea, often within sections where the primary state has no seaboard, which acts as a still more general comment on the activities described. In contrast to the often frenetic and transient acts of a consumer-oriented society, it serves as a mute reminder of permanence and space. Unlike the American countryside, it can be little encroached upon, and provides almost limitless refuge from the overcrowding of urban America, becoming a natural equivalent to the "site of aeration, of purification, of judgment," which the late Mark Rothko strove to create in his painting.[25]

Butor's use of the sea provides an excellent example of the procedure, used throughout *Mobile*, of placing different sections of text in juxtaposition in order to provide mutual commentary or contamination. Every detail of the text, he claims, has its allotted place, for reasons which he admits he is often unable to give (*Entretiens*, p. 190). In some cases—the disintegration of the ideal of fraternity, or the alliance of religion and commercialism—the process is easily identified. Elsewhere it varies from the aggressively obvious to the subtle (although this is to a considerable extent dependent on the reader's sharpness of intelligence and eye), or from the somber to the witty and ludicrous. For instance, the theme of nature versus the productions of man is also present in the form of abrupt transitions between geographical features and mail-order catalogues: "Thirsty? Drink Coca-Cola!—The Le Moine and Sangammon rivers join the Illinois,—or guinea-pigs, 'sold in pairs. Eat grass or greenstuff. No choice of color. Carriage one and a half times express freight from Greenville, Ohio' " (p. 63). Colors of man-made objects are listed alongside descriptions of natural features to create a shifting effect which can often be quite amusing: "*In the Mammoth's Cave, seven-mile guided tours:* (. . .)—or a plastic mosaic coating for your bathroom:/(. . .) *the bottomless pit,/*—burgundy,/—*the freezing of Niagara . . .* [*sic*]/caramel,/—candied lemon,/ *It's a Blacks' christening, yet another black child./*—turquoise,/ Black and White together."[26] Thomas Jefferson's denials of the Negro's esthetic sense are accompanied by details of the fanatical attention he paid to the decor of his mansion Monticello—and of his extreme meanness, since his servants doubled as musicians for no extra pay (pp. 122–23). In this way, the complexity of his character is suggested, and a further dimension is added to the theme of inequality, for the same man who proclaims the natural inferiority of the Negro is willing to exploit his (white) employees' *superior* artistic talents—but without increasing their wages. In the section on Indiana, the whole tragic history of the American Indian is unfolded in successive, italicized accounts of the richness of their civilization, William Penn's treaty with them, their massacre by militiamen, and their ultimate degradation in the "Chapel Lake Indian Ceremonials" (pp. 73–84).

The thematic importance of juxtaposition in *Mobile* varies a good deal, from the illustrations of racial and social inequality to the exploitation of ambiguity in lists, which is often thematically negligible but a powerful means of extending our imagination, Butor claims.[27] But the greatest contribution to the uniqueness of Butor's vision of America is undoubtedly the constant placing in apposition of elements whose separate introduction, while generating interest, would be incapable of producing the effects of surprise, pathos, or shock with which *Mobile* abounds: "*Like all insights of undoubted truth, this vision arises out of the harmonizing of separate elements . . . .*"[28]

III   *America and Europe*

"*Mobile* means nothing to those who haven't visited the United States at two hundred miles an hour . . ." (*sic*); this disheartened reaction of an otherwise well-disposed academic, R.-M. Albérès,[29] is a grave overestimation of the book's difficulty. To a French public reared on Mallarmé and Apollinaire, *Mobile* should not present any insuperable problems, and American readers with a knowledge of Dos Passos or William Carlos Williams ought to be on reasonably familiar ground. Nevertheless, as Roland Barthes has argued with great wit and perspicacity, one of the major reasons for the "scandale" of *Mobile* was the invasion of the sacred territory of the travel book by procedures which had only been tolerated because they had not previously transcended the bounds of poetry. Mallarmé and Apollinaire were *poets*, and even if one basically disapproved of their assault on the traditional concept of the page, it was still harmless enough, being confined to the poetic domain. As Barthes explains: "Here one detects a familiar technique of respectable societies: 'localizing' freedom, as one would lance an abcess."[30] In short, one of the greatest obstacles to the acceptance of *Mobile* was not its intrinsic difficulty but a lack of security on the part of many readers. The very foundations of the edifice of literature-as-reassurance were shaken by a work which had spilled over from poetry into travel literature and, instead of letting the eye—and the mind—be lulled by the development of ideas on successive pages, treated them in apposition, abandoned them, or returned to them, in general making one work far too hard. But for American readers, the main annoyance was caused by the irrelevant treatment of great myths, or historical figures such as

Jefferson (*Entretiens*, pp. 212–13). The importance of *Mobile* as a work of social interpretation is, I have suggested, considerable. Common themes, particularly that of the Negro's condition, are renewed by Butor's provocative treatment, and the emphasis on the often forgotten American Indian, or the importance of colors in America, is original and stimulating. Yet the greatest—although understandable—mistake of those who disliked Butor's critical treatment of past and present America was not to realize that, behind the apparent target, the real one is Western European Man.

Mobile is the culmination of the attack on our blindness, ignorance, and bigotry beginning in *Passage de Milan* and continued, with differences of emphasis, in the subsequent novels. The greed of the early Spanish conquerors of Central and South America, which blinded them to the value of the civilization they discovered and destroyed there (*Degrés*) is a relatively minor outbreak of the European *malaise* which has affected the United States ever since it was first settled. Lack of security is the root problem, with the classical consequences of aggressiveness and refusal to entertain alternative modes of thought; worse still, it is a self-perpetuating problem, since one of the primary causes is the presence within our minds of irreconcilable cultural and religious systems (*Passage de Milan*). Thus, when we come into contact with an alien way of life, the reactions already outlined occur: initially, its representatives are deported or butchered, while those remaining (if any) are "converted" with often dubious consequences, and then carefully pushed into Reservations where they can be either forgotten, or visited without danger.[31] I write this in Australia, where the record of the British settler can scarcely be better than the Spaniard's in America. Only an intelligent minority reacts in yet another manner, by welcoming the illumination of our civilization by another; Montaigne's vision of Alexander the Great "nobly" conquering America (*Degrés*) is reversed by Chateaubriand who, in his *Voyage en Amérique*, asks: "Who knows but that one day we might have seen some American Columbus landing on our shores to discover the Old World?"[32]

In its turn, Chateaubriand's vision of America as a "Fountain of Youth that will rejuvenate our decrepit civilization" is modified by Butor, who sees it, less idealistically, as a "magnifying glass" of Western civilization (*Entretiens*, p. 228). What he names the

"American guilt" has, he maintains, its roots in our own European conscience (*ibid.*, p. 233). America, by virtue of its advanced technology, its colonial history, even its size,[33] allows us to look both forward and backward: forward to the day when we will have reached the present stage of American technology and are faced with the same problems, notably the overwhelming of man by objects; backward into our own history—and guilt—since the current repression of the Indian or Negro simply mirrors our ancestors' more direct but no less disastrous treatment of colored peoples. And whether we look to the future or the past—or the present—the picture appears uniformly gloomy.

In view of Butor's highly critical interpretation of American history and contemporary life, with its implications for the whole of Western society, even the qualified optimism of the apostrophe to America at the end of *Mobile* seems unjustified:

Sleep.../ Dreams.../ America at night.../ Oh mask!/ Monster..../ Lies.../ Tremor!/ Oh land of speed.../ Source of conjunction.../ Abbey of rootlessness!/ Oh America without the bank.../ Oh America upturned!/ Oh sheaf of journeys.../ Chorus of races.../ Years and years hence.../ Will a stone be left standing?/ Unrecognizable at last recognizable./ Texture of sources!/ Throbbing beneath the transparent tissue of the States.../ The richest of poverty.../ How we await you, America!/ How we await your turning!/ How we observe you in the night! (sic, pp. 325–29)

Yet the witty, dynamic presentation of America to which both the form and content of *Mobile* contribute, suggest not so much decay as vitality. Like Balzac's *Comédie Humaine, Mobile* depicts a society which is in many ways decadent yet somehow remains intensely vigorous. In Balzac's world, fortunes are made and lost overnight, evil constantly triumphs over good, yet society continues to thrive, with no real possibility of that ultimate, all-embracing catastrophe haunting Zola's jaundiced depiction of the Second Empire—society may be morally and spiritually bankrupt, but in a paradoxically buoyant manner. *Mobile* captures a similar, vital spirit in contemporary America, which it conveys in part by the jaunty conveyance of its mainly somber message. Where there are contrasts, there is potential for change.

Herein lies the main reason for Butor's optimism. His selection and provisional arrangement of American material is calculated to provoke, even disorientate us, in order that an "onset of awareness" may follow. In this respect, the reader's path follows that of the author, who, before writing *Passage de Milan*, sought to increase the disorientation produced by a stay in Germany by next residing in Egypt—a still greater degree of bewilderment would, he hoped, be followed by an enormous increase in the ability to *compare*. Butor's solution to all our problems is both formal and syncretic: formal, in the sense that rigid organization of the matter at our disposal reveals unsuspected aspects (and produces poetry); syncretic, since it is only by encompassing a broad and contradictory range of knowledge that one can be sure of appreciating the most valuable parts. *Mobile* does not of course aim at a *totality* of knowledge about its chosen field, although one of Butor's protagonists, Pierre Vernier, attempts such a task. But it is essentially a book about Europeans in America, the relations between them, that country, and its other inhabitants. By looking at America, taking not so much a plunge in the "Fountain of Youth" as a tonic of disorientation, we may see ourselves more clearly in the American mirror and be capable of devising a new way of life (*Entretiens*, p. 199).

CHAPTER 7

Toward the "œuvre ouverte"—*I*

I *General Principles*

ALTHOUGH *Mobile* develops certain features already present in Butor's earlier works, its attempt to achieve total congruence of form and theme still produced something strikingly different from the novels, where formal research is sometimes overshadowed by content. Three books published over the next three years— *Réseau aérien, Description de San Marco,* and *6 810 000 Litres d'eau par seconde*—continue and consolidate the formal experimentation, with the last-named exploiting the possibilities of stereophony. In spite of an apparent thematic poverty alongside *Mobile,* all express, more or less obliquely, some of the familiar Butorian preoccupations, such as the problem of race in *6 810 000 Litres,* or the themes of memory and time in *San Marco.* Nevertheless, on a first reading, all appear to be rather thin variations on the theme of "poésie sur le voyage" or mobile applications of the "génie du lieu" principle: *Réseau aérien* poeticizes the impressions of air travelers; *Description de San Marco* creates a polyphony of architectural, iconographic, and verbal elements centered on St. Mark's, Venice; and *6 810 000 Litres* attempts a similar, quasimusical arrangement on the theme of the Niagara Falls.

The only recently found balance between what are traditionally called "content" and "form" thus appears to be replaced fairly rapidly by a bias in favor of the latter. Perhaps it would be more accurate to say that the full meaning of a work is invariably only deducible from the way in which language is used within it, or from its structure. Not that Butor is evolving toward a kind of "poésie pure," which is clearly anathema to him, but his writing does appear progressively more formalist.[1] For example, *6 810 000 Litres* is *about* the Niagara Falls as a modern center of pilgrimage, but one of its major themes, the decrepitude of everyday language, is not *expressed* at all, but must be inferred from Butor's treatment of various parts of the text.[2] A later work still, the "opera" *Votre*

Faust, is *about* a modern Faust, the composer Henri, who enters into a disastrous pact with an impresario (Mephistopheles); from this, one might well deduce that the status of the artist in contemporary society is being commented on, particularly as Butor has engaged in active propaganda on his behalf elsewhere.[3] Although there is nothing against such an interpretation, it misses the formal significance of *Votre Faust* as an example of collaboration—in which librettist, composer, earlier composers and poets (whose works are frequently quoted), and even the audience, which votes or interrupts, contribute to the final result. Here, formal demonstration not only takes precedence over thematic narration but actually affects its significance, since the real collaboration between all parties concerned provides a very direct commentary on the degrading relationship between *fictional* impresario and the composer, Henri.

Indeed, collaboration becomes one of the principal concerns of the post-*Mobile* period, with reader, listener, or audience participation in the "open" work being encouraged in a variety of ways, from voting in *Votre Faust* to choice of reading or listening itineraries in *6 810 000 Litres* and more restricted movement within the text in *Réseau aérien* and *San Marco*. Collaboration by proxy, in the form of extended quotation and elaboration of secondary texts, already practiced extensively in *Mobile*, is utilized systematically in *6 810 000 Litres*, *Votre Faust*, and the collection of poems entitled *Illustrations*, where Chateaubriand, Mallarmé, Goethe, Marlowe, Petrarch and Góngora are quoted.[4] *6 810 000 Litres* more modestly confines itself to two texts of Chateaubriand describing the Falls, although it pulverizes them unmercifully for the purposes of counterpoint. Finally, in the "libretto" (if it can be called this) of *Votre Faust*, most of the "contributors" to *Illustrations* reappear, along with other poets; its music and decor are an intricate amalgam of composers from Monteverdi to Webern and artists including Rembrandt and Delacroix.

But most important of all is collaboration *between* the arts. Butor is more than ever concerned to destroy barriers, not only between different branches of the same art—between novel, travel book and poetry—but between drama and opera,[5] and, more widely still, between literature, painting, music, and architecture. If the written word is still accorded primacy in a recent essay on "La Littérature, l'oreille et l'œil,"[6] its intimate relationship with the other arts and the mutual profit derived is also celebrated—in Utopian language. As always, the ultimate point of reference is reality—and its transformation—in view of which Butor's dislike of "pure" music and art for art's sake becomes clear. The two volumes of *Illustrations* are commentary poems on mainly plastic art (engravings, paintings, photographs, etc.); two other works (*6 810 000 Litres* and *Réseau aérien*) use the resources of radio for poetic ends; *San Marco* is basically a poem illustrating the relation between architecture, mosaics, and inscriptions; finally, *Votre Faust*, in theory at least, is much closer to the Wagnerian concept of a synthesis of poetry, music, and stagecraft than the Italianate marriage without the bride, where only the music matters. Butor's very latest contribution to the study of the relation between the arts is entitled *Les Mots dans la peinture*, in which a future volume on "the question of images within books" in hinted at.[7]

With the disappearance of the protagonist (except in *Votre Faust*), man's disorientation is now taken for granted, and Butor's Utopianism may appear less blatant. But it is still part of his thought and can be found in theoretical writings such as "La Littérature, l'oreille et l'œil," or articles in which he analyzes a writer's or artist's search for a "missing central Paradise" (Montaigne) or "the world upturned," a better, transformed world symbolized by the refractive power of Lake Geneva (Rousseau) or Monet's treatment of water in his painting.[8] Indeed, Butor appears to be increasingly concerned with the natural world—either directly, or via its depiction in works of art—as a source of suggestion and value, and the nearest he ever approaches a religious sentiment is in the use of external nature as a silent comment on the follies of man in *Mobile* and *6 810 000 Litres*. The last-named work and *Réseau aérien* depend very heavily on the relation between man in the foreground and a backcloth of nature for their effect, while numerous poems express in luxuriant fashion the themes of disorientation and regret, using nature as their main vehicle.[9] All of this, from the Utopianism to the ambiguous but frequent references to nature, suggests a strong Romantic vein in a man whose works have frequently been accused of hypercerebrality.

In fact, Butor is simultaneously cerebral, Utopian, formalist, *and* Romantic, although the dosage varies according to the work concerned. But less than ever, I think, does he really surprise. His

audacity is not of the turncoat variety, like that of Gautier's hero
Daniel Jovard, who changes from an archclassic into a "Jeune-
France" overnight; it is calculated and cumulative, a reasoned
assault on the bastions of traditionalism, gathering formal momentum as it invests its enemy. More than ever, his remark to Georges
Charbonnier that: "When I consider the books I've already written,
I have the feeling that they're nearly all the same" (*Entretiens*, p.
99) appears true. From *Passage de Milan* to *Votre Faust*, the
impression that one is reading the same work, in spite of immense
differences in form and even genre, is overwhelming. This may be
some justification for a certain amount of repetition in the analyses
that follow.

II Réseau aérien

Réseau aérien, subtitled *texte radiophonique* (Gallimard, 1962),
attracted extremely little attention when it was published, mainly
because it was overshadowed by *Mobile*, which appeared earlier
the same year, and whose technique it applies—both less ambi-
tiously and less successfully—to the medium of broadcasting. The
majority of those who have come into contact with it will have
done so via the O.R.T.F., by whom it was commissioned, and then
first broadcast on June 16, 1962.

Its main theme and over-all structure are basically simple,
although the following analysis may not give that impression.
There are ten actors or voices, five of whom are male (A, B, C, D,
E) and the rest female (f, g, h, i, j). Two couples leave Paris for
New Caledonia on different planes and by different routes, one
flying via Athens, Teheran, Karachi, Bangkok, and Saigon, and
the other by the Western route, via Canada, mainland America,
and Honolulu. The couples in each plane (usually of the opposite
sex) are given fragments of dialogue comprising six remarks and
six replies, seldom more than a sentence long.

When a plane lands, a couple leaves it and is not replaced,[10] while
a new plane takes off, bound in the opposite direction, and having
on board only one couple to begin with. Plane one thus deposits
couple B-j at its first stop, Athens, as plane three takes off for Orly
with couple C-i on board.[11] A total of ten planes is involved, but
no more than seven are ever airborne at the same time, since several

start and finish their journeys while others are still heading for their
final destination: plane three (Athens-Orly) only appears for a very
short while, whereas plane seven (Los Angeles-Montreal-Orly) has
considerably more distance to cover and consequently occupies
much more of the text. In short, the whole operation is governed by
the principle that what goes up must come down, the book ending
when planes one and two have reached Nouméa and nine and ten
Orly.[12]

Like many of Butor's works, *Réseau aérien* increases in complication and gathers poetic momentum; early on, touch-downs are
frequent, governed by the simple fact that, for instance, the distance
between Paris and Athens is less than that between Paris and
Montreal, whereas later there are more planes airborne and greater
distances to be covered. At the same time, Butor has chosen to keep
even the short-haul planes aloft, if poetically necessary, and pages
72 to 90, with six airborne simultaneously, contain the most lyrical
and hallucinatory passages in the entire work. Although the *reader*
can to some extent organize his itinerary, as in *Mobile*, by following
individual couples, or planes, or simply reading from beginning to
end, the first two methods are unrewarding, since either the conversations are for the most part uninteresting or meaningless, or the
plane concerned may land after a few pages. None of these possibilities are in any case open to the listener. *Réseau aérien* only impresses
if read in a normal, successive manner, for it is only then that the
increasingly poetic language, the rhythm of dialogues, the leitmotives, the practice of assonance, alliteration, and juxtaposition, may
be appreciated. The climax is reached a few pages before the end,
when both monotony and anxiety are intermingled, after which
the tone becomes calmer as the touch-downs at Orly and Nouméa
approach. As an example of crescendo, *Réseau aérien* is impressive.

Its general effect is similar to that produced by *Mobile*: nothing
is fixed, except the reader or listener, acting as a kind of mental
control tower, receiving and to some extent organizing impressions
from all over the globe. The carefully planned structure is of course
not gratuitous,[13] but an original means of conveying the kaleidoscope
of passengers' impressions and emotions—trepidation, relief, regret,
inability to forget—and the over-all rhythm of modern air travel: the
recurrence of certain planes on pages 72 to 90 (Planes 9, 7, 2, 10, 8;
1, 9, 7, 2, 10, 8; 1, 9, 7, 2, 10, 8; 1, 9, 7, 2, 10, 8) with the attendant

repetition of obsessional themes, produces an effect of hallucination, monotony, and lassitude, Most important of all, the interchangeability of dialogues created by the juxtaposition of virtually anonymous passengers allows the early *lieux communs* to merge gradually into a kind of collective poem.[14] Less than ever does the individual response to experience seem to concern Butor.

The dialogues begin in a deliberately banal way, with the casual chatter of air travelers (p. 11). But even early on, the common preoccupations of nearly all the couples, either with what awaits them, or what they have left behind, is expressed. Couple A-j in plane one, who appear to be emigrant schoolteachers (p. 14), are at first curious rather than worried: "What will Noumea be like? / We'll soon get settled" (p. 14); later, however, when the long journey, night, and fitful sleep take their effect, the conversation evolves into a kind of litany:

A   Sleep. Are you sleeping? You dream, you tremble, you open your eyes, you move your lips.
j   Where are we? clasp me, hold me!
A   We have crossed the equator, entering the other side of the earth where the seasons are reversed.
j   Dry my tears.
A   Your tears?
j   I am drunk with the moonlight's rain streaming from all these enormous leaves that stroke me, from all these enormous flowers that caress me and make me shut my eyes. I close my eyes again, I sleep, I dream, you carry me, you clasp me, you gently dry my tears with your lips. You carry me in your arms, you carry me across pools, and you splash me with tepid drops. (pp. 82–83)

Along with the development of private thoughts into a more generalized poetic chant (as happens in *Passage de Milan* and *Mobile*), the theme of nature as a contrast to, or illustration of, the dominant concerns of man grows in importance. A few early remarks about the sky or land (e.g., pp. 16, 18), which are no more than stock tokens of admiration typical of people blessed with just a little imagination, rapidly give way to a much more poetic form of dialogue:

C   Tea?
i   Yes please, tea.
C   The sunset.
i   Pursuing the sun.

C   The green sky.   *(plane 3)*
i   Above the dark green sea.

A   The dazzling sky.   *(plane 2)*
i   The dazzling sun.
A   The hours go by but not the day.
i   Hollows in the plain of clouds.
A   They seem brimming with thick, turbulent mud. (p. 20)

In this extract, nearly all the techniques used by Butor later on in
Réseau aérien are present: the "snapshot" ("Hollows in the plain of
clouds"); alliteration and assonance ("vert/mer" [green/sea], "ciel/
soleil" [sky/sun]; and juxtaposition in dialogues to convey the effects
of the same basic elements on different couples ("The green sky/ The
dazzling sky"). On occasions, juxtaposition can lead to (presumably
deliberate) incongruity: [The sunrise] "Catching the mountains'
heights (. . . .) Their summits crests of golden cocks./By-passing their
amber névé, their glaciers of white wine./The plane isn't moving about
any more. I'm hungry" (pp. 44–45). But usually, particularly in the
later stages of the book, images of nature as an indication of man's
disorientation appear:

A   *Moon rising over the shores of Borneo.*
j   *The forest, your forest, the moon in your forest.*
A   *Are you asleep? Sleep in this forest, I'll carry you in this forest.*
j   *So dense, so unknown, so alive with snakes.*
A   *With snakes' eyes, snakes' hissings, volcanoes' rumblings, snapping
     of birds' beaks.* (p. 79)[15]

Two leitmotives give added coherence to *Réseau aérien*, particularly
as they are interrelated: the minerals found in New Caledonia (nickel,
gold ["or"], iron, copper, chromium, coal) and the phoenix.[16] The
first is introduced by couple A-i on plane two; the husband appears
to have business in the mines (p. 115), and the names of the various
minerals run alliteratively through their heads (p. 47). "Phénix" is
introduced, naturally enough, through image association in connection with the sun (p. 67). The two themes are combined on several
occasions, when A-i on plane two reminisces about the mines in
Noumea (p. 71), or when the same couple addresses a farewell to the
long Pacific night from which they are just emerging: "*Adieu,
phoenix! / Dark phoenix in ashes. / Adieu long night of Pacific
Springtime, mine-shaft. / And now the long night, the gentle night*

of Pacific autumn. / Close nickel of dawn. / Phoenix" (pp. 80–81).

As the text unfolds, its structural complication is revealed by the dense network of images. The one word "Clouds," which opens the dialogues of plane seven (p. 71), is taken up and expanded two pages later: "Clouds, unending clouds, white, marvellous, storm-tossed," followed, almost immediately, by "Water, unending, naked water, lost water, green and white" (plane seven, p. 73), which develops into "Mile upon mile of dark water between that town and us" (plane ten, p. 74), with the themes of water and clouds combining just a little later: "Water, unending water, unending clouds, unending, shifting shapes" (p. 76). Then, a new, but similarly obsessive theme line emerges: "Hour upon hour . . ." (p. 77), which is interrupted in its turn by the opening of the next three groups of dialogue, grouped around the themes of "sun," "moon," and "day" (pp. 78–79). It returns on page 81, only to be supplanted by "Mile upon mile. . . ." The dominant effect produced is of the immense monotony of long-distance air travel, and it is at this stage that the dreams, insistent memories, and obsessive thoughts are most prominent.

This repetition of what might be called *elemental* vocabulary—earth, sky, sun-phoenix, moon, water, clouds, simple colors, particularly black and gold—is one of the most striking characteristics of *Réseau aérien*. As plane ten approaches Orly, a series of elliptical phrases concentrates on three dominant elements, "or" (gold), "nuit" (night), and "nuées" (clouds) (pp. 118–19): Given Butor's interest in alchemy,[17] it is presumably not unintended that the arrival at *Or*-ly by one group of travelers, with the attendant repetition of "or," coincides with the arrival of others in New Caledonia, land of base metals. This is not to suggest that the entire work is an exercise in alchemical symbolism, rather that it illustrates Butor's frequent use of mythical or mystical themes in order to underline the complexity of the world and illuminate man's behavior in it. By a hint of alchemical myth, he is emphasizing the delight—and cupidity—of those returning to Paris after long, dreary years spent in the Far East.[18] Conversely, the despair of j in plane one, arriving in New Caledonia, is deepened by the fact that she is on the very periphery of the French community and that the struggle to return to Paris will be hard, involving numerous stages.[19]

If this appears rather facile, a good deal of the rest of *Réseau aérien* may also seem gratuitous. There are of course many successful and quite striking fragments of dialogue, often brought about by an unusual view of land, sea, or clouds: "Clouds have suddenly parted, it's like a path./ Purple beech./ Like a great glowing maple in the direction of Europe./ The sea nourished by black sap./ And the boat you can see as if beyond dead leaves, already all lit up./ Mahogany moiré changing into violet" (p. 34); or: "New skies of snow./ Névés of clouds./ Clouds of ice on the coasts./ Glaciers floating in the sky" (p. 105). But in spite of the careful architecture, the links and repetitions of imagery, the alliteration and assonance, there is a poetic looseness about the work which is less a consequence of any failure of inspiration than of Butor's conception of poetry itself as a kind of "trying out" of elements in juxtaposition. The disquieting signs of gratuitousness in *L'Emploi du temps* also recur in *Mobile*, but in neither work do they attract much attention because of the thematic richness largely submerging them. But if, as here, there is less recognizable content to divert the mind, then it quite naturally focuses on "forme." While this is not the place for a generalized discussion of Butor's use of language, which can be found in Chapter 8, *Réseau aérien* does provide an interesting sample of his failings in this domain.

Chief among these is the lavish employment of alliteration, assonance, repetition, and juxtaposition to achieve an effect of sonorousness or harmony alone, with any meaning running a poor second to the overpowering succession of sounds. More crudely put, parts of the text sound like a jingle, thus: "*Au Jardin des Plantes,/ Nous irons reconnaître les oiseaux de l'Inde./ Dans le soir, dans la soie du soir, la moire du soir./ Dans l'eau ruisse- lante d'un soir de lune*" (p. 103) ["In the Jardin des Plantes,/ We will recognize the birds of India./ In the evening, in the silk of the evening, the moiré of the evening./ In the streaming water of a moonlit evening."], where the cascade of sibilants and "oi" sounds is a rather facile manner of suggesting softness and calm. A related weakness is a gratuitous kind of preciosity, which in *Réseau aérien* assumes such forms as: "Tu retrouveras cette dent de lune à jamais cariée des nuits de là-bas" (p. 74), ["You'll see that tooth-like piece of moon permanently rotted by those Noumean nights"], or involves simple image association such as: "All the wines were running in the clouds (. . . .) The sea of Guinness and black coffee" (p. 111), which is a possible reminiscence of part of Rimbaud's "Comédie de la soif," although it lacks that poem's coarse vitality. In all these cases, internal necessity has been sacrificed to the production of a general effect, and the density and *total* interplay of elements characteristic of the best poetry is lacking. Elsewhere, the sheer ordinariness of the text disappoints: "Mountains the color of tea./ Mountain shadows the color of heliotrope./ Mountain snows the color of white women./ Whom the sun is beginning to bronze" (p. 75). A convincing demonstration that new *forms* are necessitated by a new field of exploration (here, air travel), *Réseau aérien* persuades us less readily that poetry inevitably follows their use.

III *Monument solide*—Description de San Marco[20]

One of the many forces assailing man in the hostile world Butor depicts is time. In two novels, *L'Emploi du temps* and *Degrés*, it is one of several factors in the heroes' failure; it does not play a significant part in the other two novels, nor in *Mobile*, although its passing is symbolized in *6 810 000 Litres* by the flow of water over the Niagara Falls. Indeed, throughout Butor's work, the link between time, water, and literal or figurative erosion is established in a manner which clearly owes much to Gaston Bachelard: Bleston's ceaseless rain is part of the "realistic" decor, saps Revel's willpower, and acts as a poetic token of the amnesia always threatening him. Nevertheless, the erosive force of time is compensated, for Butor, by its very existence. In all the exemplary works, the movement is toward the future; the dimension of time is necessary for change to occur, and the inconclusiveness of his protagonists' struggle creates a kind of void synonymous with potentiality. In *Description de San Marco*, however, it is not the future that concerns Butor, but the present, and the challenge of time and literal erosion is met in a different manner. The permanence of St. Mark's, constantly threatened, like the city it dominates, by the sea,[21] is celebrated by a "polyphonie spatiale" (text, p. 77) in which the counterpoint of "eau/or" ["water/gold"] symbolizes the eternal battle between solidity and erosion. On this occasion, the basilica wins, preserved in the "temporary tomb" of Butor's book which, when opened, provides a stimulant for the reader's memories:

The whole of this text is designed to be illustrated by the monument itself, and can only take on all its properties when it is steeped in it as in a liquid. Until then, may it act as a foretaste, a stimulant, and then, steeped in the images which it will have helped to emerge against the background of gold and shadow, may it restore all your memories that are lovingly encompassed by its pages [back cover].

As well as being a homage to the basilica, *Description de San Marco* also celebrates the eightieth birthday of Igor Stravinsky, whose "Canticum sacrum ad honorem Sancti Marci nominis" was first performed at Venice in 1956, and respects the memory of the Englishman John Ruskin, one of the most sensitive persons ever to have set foot in St. Mark's. Ruskin's *The Stones of Venice* and the chapter edited by him in *St. Mark's Rest*[22] are at once very similar to and markedly different from Butor. The main similarity lies in the importance both authors attach to the inscriptions. In the words of Ruskin, lamenting our present-day familiarity and weariness with writing: "the old architect was sure of readers. He knew that every one would be glad to decipher all that he wrote; that they would rejoice in possessing the vaulted leaves of his stone manuscript; and that the more he gave them, the more grateful would the people be." (*SV*, p. 133).[23]

Although Ruskin describes all parts of the basilica with considerable thoroughness, it is the baptistery which receives most detailed treatment. As Butor examines this part of St. Mark's in considerable detail as well, a comparison of his text and Ruskin's may help to illuminate both methods.[24]

At the outset of his description, Ruskin warns against a haphazard itinerary (*SMR*, pp. 309–10) which fails to connect the subjects of the mosaics, and he concludes it with a reminder of the way in which the different parts of the baptistery are related to each other (pp. 333–34). Each cycle of mosaics is thus visited in strict order, from the altar-piece, focal point of the whole chapel, followed by the life of St. John the Baptist, its principal theme, to a series of other subjects, ending with Christ and the angels. The treatment of each subject or cycle is very similar, consisting of a description of variable length, a faithful quotation of the accompanying (often severely abbreviated) inscription, followed by the full biblical quotation and an English translation. The vertical order of these elements is somewhat varied, the description preceding or following the quotation, and the horizontal disposition is also changed on occasion, producing several very Butorian pages utilizing not only italic and roman, but three sizes of type and three columns of text! But the order of visit is never allowed to vary; the author is always at our elbow, guiding us to the next stage: "The visitor has thus examined all the mosaics except those of the three domes. He must now, therefore, return from near the altar at the further end of the chapel, and take first the vaulting ... of that part of the roof" (*SMR*, p. 326). By the end of the chapter, the reader will have absorbed a good deal of information, successively and interestingly presented, relating almost exclusively to the mosaics and inscriptions. If he has visited St. Mark's, certain memories (of these two aspects) will be directly stimulated, while others may be brought back by association.

Butor presents his reader with a far wider range of experience, simultaneously rather than successively, through which the primary stimulation will be direct. If the most important feature of the baptistery for him remains the mosaics and inscriptions, the crowd inside and reminders of Venice outside are also treated, although an aspect present in other sections—the relation between the mosaics' subject matter and the history of Venice—is missing. The usual methods of indentation and italicizing are used to separate the different facets of the text; the crowd's babble runs, appropriately enough, right across the page, from the extreme left-hand margin to the extreme right, and is italicized; starting in the next margin, Butor's general commentary on the baptistery's architecture, the mosaics, and the scene through the door is given, while the narrowest portion of the page is concerned with impressions (rather than detailed descriptions) of the mosaics, quotation of the inscriptions and—as with Ruskin—the full biblical text relevant to them.

Compared with the minute, orderly catalogue of *St. Mark's Rest*, Butor's impressions seem both haphazard and incomplete, ignoring totally certain scenes, concentrating on unimportant facets of others, and darting about with no respect for continuity.[25] Herein lies of course the main difference between Butor and Ruskin. With the exception of his emphasis on the close relationship between mosaics and inscriptions, the latter treats the various aspects of St. Mark's— its origins, architecture, and place in Venetian history—systematically and *successively*. Butor is far more concerned to set up "resonances" between all these aspects, and others, so that the relations between them shall be available to the reader *simultaneously*. This difference can also be seen in the authors' respective treatment of the contrast between the cosmopolitan and largely indifferent crowd and the edifice on which they converge. As Ruskin emphasizes: "Men met there from all the countries of the earth, for traffic or for pleasure, but, above the crowd swaying for ever to and fro in the restlessness of avarice or thirst of delight, was seen perpetually the glory of the temple . . . (*SV*, p. 140). Butor also stresses the contrast (which for Ruskin clearly has religious overtones), but goes a step further: a bastion of splendor against indifference and erosion by time, the basilica participates in a kind of dialogue with the crowd milling in and around it, by means of a series of correspondences set up between its mosaics and the tourists' mode of dress.[26]

Saint Mark's is obviously an excellent subject for Butor, since of all the monuments of the Western world, it is perhaps the most covered in inscriptions (Butor, p. 26). It is also one of the most frequented, with all the indifference and admiration thereby implied; finally, the life and death of St. Mark himself, commemorated in the mosaics, is inextricably linked with Venice and its history. Thus, on every page, architecture and mosaics, inscriptions and words, stones and living beings, past and present, all are linked by Butor's polyphony:

> . . . and higher still, the
> summit of the façade, the
> Evangelist again blessing, the
> light or the rain streaming
> over the pages he holds open.
>
> Streaming from page to page, from book to
> book, from text to image, from crowd of
> stone to crowd of flesh.
>
> *italian* [*sic*] . . . —*An orange juice.*—*And you, where are you
> staying?*—*I'd like . . . —I'd prefer . . . —The gondola!. . . .
> Look at that necklace of orange pearls, no,*
>
> Angels surrounding the Saint carrying
> censers; the crowd's murmur transmuted,
> as it reaches them, into gentle whiffs
> of vapor. (*sic*, p. 23)

The kaleidoscope of colors inside the basilica is described both directly and obliquely through snatches of tourists' conversation, which is frequently not concerned with the surrounding marvels at all: "*That woman in an indigo dress.* / (. . .) / *Gold.* [*sic*] / (. . .)/ *Pink.* / (. . .) / *Shadow*" (p. 93); the subjects of mosaics and Venetian history are related whenever possible: " 'Then Jehovah fashioned Man out of clay,' version of particular interest for Venice, the birth of Man being linked with the separation of clay and water, with the formation of the Venetian Archipelago" (p. 31), "Water./ Moses: taken from the water./ Venice rising out of the water. / Coffin from the waters of Egypt containing the body of Saint Mark" (p. 60); past and present are juxtaposed by citing Vasari on the commercialization of the basilica and the conversations of modern tourists seeking cheap souvenirs (p. 111).

Through all these contrasts, parallels, and cross-references, runs the theme of "eau/or," with the gold of the building and its mosaics contrasting with the erosion by sea, time, and forgetfulness:

> A cupola glimpsed between two
> glasses of fruit juice.
> A flood of people flowing past . . .
> —*Hey!*—*Monsieur! Monsieur! Do you want a good photo . . .*
> The murmur of all this . . . the distant sound
> of water . . .
> Between the wings of a pigeon in
> flight, a small belfry in gold and
> lead/.(*sic,* p. 11)[27]

Description de San Marco is a hopeful rather than Utopian book, a token of Butor's faith in the esthetic sense and determination inspiring man to erect and embellish monuments like St. Mark's, which spur successive writers or illustrators to further creation: the author of *Le Temps retrouvé* joins Ruskin on the back cover of *San Marco*, along with a long procession of unnamed, creative "readers" of the basilica to whom Butor pays homage. But we should note that his final respects are paid to the ordinary reader, final link in the long chain of collaboration who may one day add his humble stone to the edifice of literature, which is the ultimate guarantee of both preservation and change:

> Accept this homage as it stands,
> dear reader who seeks to listen and see,
> DESCRIPTION DE SAN MARCO
> Michel Butor

IV *Monument liquide*—6 810 000 Litres d'eau par seconde[28]

Butor's exploration of the "génie du lieu" continues in his next major work, a poetic presentation of the history, myth, and physical presence of the Niagara Falls in relation to the different itineraries and emotions of the endless stream of tourists who visit them each year. On this occasion, the visitors do not surge round a solid monument, symbol of triumph over passing time, but are echoed, mocked, and, on occasion, literally swallowed up by the immense flow of the Falls, within a temporal framework whose main characteristic is acceleration. Fading memories, regret, and nostalgia form an increasing part of a journey from spring to the depths of winter, in the course of which one of the most depressing themes of *Mobile*, racial disharmony, is taken up once more. *6 810 000 Litres* is a somber book, only partly relieved by flashes of incongruous humor, and appears totally devoid of the Utopianism of *Mobile* or the exaltation of man's creative powers in *San Marco*.

The production of the work's tone and effect depends even more on an over-all structural pattern, making Butor's previous excursion into the realm of broadcasting seem simple by comparison. In place of a theoretical choice of itineraries for the reader and none for the listener, the stereophonic principle of *6 810 000 Litres* allows the former up to ten different routes within its twelve sections and thirty-four parentheses,[29] while the listener, by a simple adjustment of controls, can decide which sounds or voices he wishes to hear or suppress. Even the producer is completely free to choose which of the alternative arrangements he will broadcast, and with unlimited time he could presumably utilize them all. In order to make full use of the stereophony, Butor has disposed background noises, both man-made and natural, to the left, right, or centrally; a central "speaker" (*sic*) gives a uniformly loud commentary on the scene and appears to double as a guide in section ten; a central "lecteur" reads out, more softly, two texts of Chateaubriand, and voices of deliberately stereotyped and interchangeable couples (the parallel with *Réseau aérien* is obvious), as well as unmarried or widowed people, are heard on the left or right.[30] Butor himself makes a brief guest appearance in the last section, as a homesick Frenchman, "*visiting professor* à l'université de Buffalo."

The book is further complicated by the theme and variations, consisting of two texts of Chateaubriand: the description of the Niagara Falls in the *Essai historique, politique et moral sur les révolutions anciennes et modernes* of 1797, and a shorter, modified version in *Atala*. They run from beginning to end, are interwoven with the rest of the text, and are subjected to ruthless deformation. If the word "juxtaposition" has been used in abundance elsewhere, other terms are more appropriate here and are suggested by the playing of J. S. Bach's chorale "Von Himmel Hoch" as background to the December section: fugue and polyphony.[31]

In the exposition of Butor's fugue (section one: "Présentation"), the subject (Chateaubriand's text) and countersubject (speaker's description of present-day Niagara) are stated. In the development, subject and countersubject are connected by episodes or "divertissements" (the various parentheses) in which the latter is complicated by the addition of voices; later on, the themes overlap still further (principle of "stretti") until, in the last section, entitled "Coda," a dominant theme is restated (the *Atala* text is given for the first time in its entirety),[32] with the main countersubject as the theme of change. Chateaubriand's texts are subjected to rigid development and rhythmic variation throughout the work,[33] becoming a musical equivalent of the Falls, suggesting in their development, repetition, and continuous presence, the endless flow of water, which in turn symbolizes the passing of time. But they also serve another purpose, contrasting with other voices to provide a frequently ironical comment on the activities described. In "Présentation," the 1797 text clashes with the countersubject—the jumble of motels and hotels surrounding the site—in a preliminary indication of man's defilement of natural beauty: nowadays the Falls are a rendez-vous for honeymooners and lost-weekenders, a source of income for hoteliers and souvenir sellers. Man's commercial ingenuity has of course risen to the challenge of the Falls in a variety of ways, producing "Falls flags, Falls plates, Falls calendars," and, final triumph, "little naked earthenware women with detachable salt- and pepper-pot breasts" (p. 23). Elsewhere, the comments can be both sharp and humorous, as in the following extract, where a group of tourists, among them a black couple and "mutton dressed as lamb" with "gigolo," visit the "Bridal Veil":

ELMER   We're the only Blacks.
(Speaker, continuing description of tourists in protective capes) in pyjamas among these normal men wearing jackets and shoes.
FLOSSIE   I can see some young black married couples coming back, it's all right.
(reader)   *The cataract.*
ANDREW   ("just married" [*sic*]), all right?
GERTRUDE   ("mutton dressed as lamb") I'm crazy.
reader   it's less a river than a turbulent, impetuous sea [or "mother": "mer/mère"]. (p. 79)[34]

A further irony is introduced by the fact that the black gardeners are responsible for the enumeration of flower colors (which play a particularly important part in May and June) rather than the white visitors, largely bound up in their own personal and material affairs.[35] However, the latter are disturbed from their own preoccupations by the physical proximity of the "blacks" and the ensuing embarrassment in the form of memories of unpleasant encounters with them, or by the chore of buying something for a colored servant. The "old couple," visiting the Falls in the vain task of recapturing their lost youth, reminisce about the early days of marriage, when penury forced them to live in a "street of Blacks," with its inevitable smell (pp. 30–32); another white couple try to convince themselves that, after all, they don't know a pair of black people whom they glimpse (pp. 52–54); two Negroes remember with scorn the cheap shirt which their employer sent them as a present, and which they used for rags, while a white couple hunt halfheartedly for the same object to give to their black gardener (pp. 86–89). Even behind the choice of pastel colors for the illumination of the Falls there lies an ulterior motive, believes Butor: "Color can express violence, and there's a kind of homeopathic treatment by pale colors, by pastel shades, that plays a part in the Niagara illuminations" (*Entretiens*, p. 179).

But such reminders of one of the most unpleasant themes of *Mobile* are incidental compared with the generalized deterioration within the book. The time scheme accelerates relentlessly, from the one hour covered by the "Présentation" to the breathless eleven hours of the Coda, the increase in speed being underlined by the speaker's "The hour goes by.... The night goes by.... The month goes by.... The years go by," which punctuates

the text. From the cheerfulness of May and June mornings ablaze
with tulips and roses, the seasons change until a dark, frozen
March with no promise of a spring to follow is reached. To
the "old couple" and newlyweds of the early sections are
added middle-aged women and their lovers, seducers and their
prey, lonely young men and women and finally, at the onset of
winter, widows and widowers. The theme of solitude predominates at Christmas, in a painfully sentimental tableau involving
people who are either widowed or alone, with a background
of blizzards, "Von Himmel Hoch," and the frequently repeated
"broken corpses" from *Atala.* In February, the refrain "of
former days/today" predominates, against a background evoking
intense cold (p. 265).

The final deterioration occurs in the realm of language. Earlier
in the work Butor had stressed the lack of meaningful communication between his couples in a variety of ways: by emphasizing
their incompatibility, frequently resulting in quarrels, by treating
them as if they were alone (a "stage direction" for the October section reads: "All the couples are 'divorced' here; each character
speaks as if he were alone," p. 147), or by the sheer interchangeable
banality of their remarks. But almost at the end, the banality
degenerates into incoherence: "Do you think, do . . . / Everything
has changed. / What were you saying?/Me?/Yes, you of course./
I said something? / I thought. / I don't know " (*sic,* p. 280). If this
phenomenon may be explained as a linguistic betrayal of the
characters' inability to adapt to reality-in-flux, its occurrence at
the end of *6 810 000 Litres* appears to cast a gloomy retrospective
light on a book which is already unusually somber for Butor, and
wherein the use of language, according to Georges Raillard,
demonstrates "the decay of the system of representation, which
reveals the defeat and the death of a society."[36]

Yet the book is not *quite* concluded by these fragments of
conversation, since they are followed by the final sentence of
Chateaubriand's *Atala* text, quoted in full for the first time. While
it would be futile to deny the *thematic* pessimism of *6 810 000
Litres,* Chateaubriand's descriptions of the Falls are used, I believe,
for two diametrically opposed purposes (quite apart from their
contrapuntal value). The first, which we have already encountered,
is to suggest the relentless flight of time. But this end is achieved by

a virtuoso distortion, fragmentation and final reassembly, in a coherent but *different* form, of Chateaubriand's text. In this process, all stages in the development of language in general, as Butor sees it, are reflected. Language begins by presenting a false appearance of stability, which in fact is merely an indication of its fixed nature and the gap beginning to open between it and an evolving society; then, as the gap widens, disintegration occurs (the linguistic "organization in the process of being destroyed"); finally, a new organization, which is inevitably constituted by the elements of the old, is created by the "avant-garde" writer. In other words, the transmutation of the *Essai* description into the modified *Atala* version is an act of faith by which Butor demonstrates and affirms the power of *his* language. Although "disintegration" is the main characteristic of the couples' unhappy and largely uncommunicative dialogues, Butor's homage to Chateaubriand becomes a celebration of the essential quality of language: potentiality. This, and the appeal to the reader's and listener's discrimination by the "open" construction, constitute a formal invitation to share his optimism which is both subtler and more convincing than the Utopian endings of some previous works.

V Votre Faust

. In 1961, Butor met the young Belgian serialist composer, Henri Pousseur, who proposed to him the subject of Faust for a joint work whose title indicates its very tenuous link with traditional opera: *Votre Faust, fantaisie variable, genre opéra* [*"Your Faust, variable opera-type fantasy"*].[37] The history of this extraordinary production is almost as complicated as its form. It has never been published *in toto,* that is, with all the variants brought together, although extracts are in publications as diverse as the *NRF, Médiations,* the Belgian magazine and cataloguer's nightmare, *L'VII,* the *Cahiers Renaud-Barrault,* and the *Cahiers du centre d'études et de recherches marxistes* (abbreviated hereafter to *Cahiers*).[38] But although parts of the text of *Votre Faust* found a ready home in many magazines, presenting it on the stage was more difficult. Nothing came of plans to put it on at the 1964 Venice festival, and it was not until December, 1966, that the music only was performed in Brussels, entitled "Portail de Votre Faust." Finally, on January 15, 1969, the opera had its world premiere at La Piccola Scala, Milan, attracting little attention, and most of that hostile or reserved. In *Le Monde* (January 22), Jacques Lonchampt, who had already expressed his "anxiety" in reviewing the "Portail," praised the attempt but admitted his total confusion after the first vote. Above all, he wrote, there was no "profound necessity governing the performance" to convey its technical audacity: nobody cared whether Henri went to the fair with the heroine, Maggy, or not. In the *Figaro littéraire* (January 27), Maurice Fleuret combined sharpness with regret: "There is . . . something tragic in this unhappy jumble, in this muddle of so much ingenuity and talent." In spite of this near-disaster, Butor still has sufficient faith in the work to want to publish an integral version, although he has not yet resolved the technical difficulties of such an enterprise.

Butor's rôle in the preparation of *Votre Faust* has hardly been that of the traditional librettist, who sometimes barely counted once the music was written. Over the nine-year period of their collaboration, he has frequently been responsible for the selection and disposition of a good deal of the music, and Pousseur has influenced the "libretto." On a theoretical level, there has also been a good deal of reciprocal influence; Pousseur's ideas and knowledge can be traced in Butor's increasingly frequent articles on music, while the composer's greatest debt to Butor lies in his acceptance and consequent putting into musical practice of the notion of quotation. Pousseur even *talks* like Butor, if parts of the confusing *Cahiers* are correctly attributed. At all events, their general ideas on music, art, and the relation of both to reality, are now remarkably similar.

The starting point for both, without which *Votre Faust* would not have been possible, is the belief that there is no such thing as "pure" music. For Butor, it is a "realistic art," capable of transforming life;[39] if Pousseur's approach is more technical, it is based on the same premises. Speaking in an interview of Stockhausen's desire to eliminate all associations of ideas from his music, he claims that precisely the opposite has occurred in pieces like "Gesang der Jünglinge" or "Kontakte": "For one cannot kill meaning, one cannot suppress all terms of reference." As for his own work, he maintains in the same interview, it has evolved steadily toward a more significant, expressive form, especially since meeting Butor.[40] To this basic belief, Butor adds the further one that the expressive function of music is best realized in conjunction with other arts, especially drama. The present separation of dramatic art and opera is artificial, when viewed in the light of history, he maintains, while even the symphony concert is really an operatic form *manqué*: "In every symphonic concert there is a submerged opera. But also in any theatrical production without music."[41] Present-day developments in means of reproduction and communication, he continues, have rendered the separation even more absurd. If opera and theater are to have any chance of a genuine renascence, it can only be brought about by their close collaboration.

The chief expressive function of music is to convey and create *relations*, a Butorian concept expressed by Pousseur in a lecture given in Brussels just after the premiere of "Portail de Votre Faust," and justified in equally Butorian terms by reference to the "new informational milieu" which surrounds us, composed of a confusing network of images of all kinds, written, photographic, musical, advertising:

It is by becoming aware of this network that we can know where we are situated. Should we deplore this multiplicity, this fragmentation, this mixture? Or rather should we attempt to master it, to take advantage of it and, to this end, start by adapting ourselves to it, by understanding the possibilities inherent in this new, scattered system of communication, so that a more harmonious relation between it and us should prevail? (*Cahiers,* p. 13)

The answer to these two rhetorical questions forms the mainstay of *Votre Faust:* the use of quotation. As Pousseur explains elsewhere, "we accept being within a collective creative network, we accept being only an aspect, only an agent of creation. We accept the fact that the work is not simply our work but the work of a whole current of creation of which we are, at a given moment, the catalyst" (*Cahiers*, p. 38). It will be seen that "information" has here been replaced by "creation." The transition can be explained in terms of twiddling the knob of a radio or altering the channel of a television, which can be idle and confusing, or active and stimulating. In the first case, we receive a meaningless jumble of sounds, in the second, we can pass from the Beatles to Tchaikovsky (Pousseur's example) and compare them. By extension of this principle, a combination of previous musical and literary treatments of the

Faust theme, from single notes to whole scenes, will come close to encompassing its totality, and, with the selection made by the audience, produce a dynamic, "open" kind of representation.

This in its turn inevitably raises the whole question of control and chance in *Votre Faust*. It has been called "aleatory" (by Lonchampt in his review of the "Portail"), but, as Henri Pousseur has made clear, there are certain limits beyond which randomness becomes unacceptable:

J.Y. Bosseur—Is *Votre Faust* an open work?
H. Pousseur—It is at once open and closed. Cage contrasted the idea of indetermination and the determinism of our Western music; I feel that this leads to total indifferentiation, to a lack of significance, of interest. It leads to a levelling out, to an "entropy" (to use a term of information theorists) because there is no co-ordination, no organization. But in this decision of Cage there was a very important point, the liberation from the over-tight yoke of Western determinism. In Europe we have gradually tried to apply ourselves, not to indetermination, but to the creation of determinations— complex, multiple—which allow great scope for interpretation. That is to say that one is faced with works that are as determined as Classical works, and as variable as those of Cage. (*Cahiers*, p. 16)

From this, and another more sophisticated piece,[42] it is clear that although Pousseur welcomes the dynamic as opposed to the completely "fixed" concept of representation, the fear of a lapse into indifferentiation if the work is abandoned totally to chance causes him to seek a compromise. Organization is still of vital importance— elsewhere in the *Cahiers* he speaks of the indispensability to the composer of "a desire for rigor in construction" (p. 46)—but within the "open" work there is potential for alternative development, thanks to the provision for audience participation (p. 17). Not surprisingly, Butor's views are similar (*Cahiers*, p. 17).

The cautious tenor of Pousseur's remarks suggests that, on Umberto Eco's scale of "openness," from the traditional work which cannot avoid ambiguity,[43] to the experiments of Stockhausen and others, *Votre Faust* would be some distance from the most "advanced" end. Whether it is closer than, for instance, *Mobile*, is difficult to say; *Mobile* can be read line by line, just as the spectator of *Votre Faust* can presumably refuse to vote without being thrown out of the concert hall; conversely, *Mobile* does not present its openness as unequivocally as *Votre Faust*. In relation to Eco's ideal ("the possibility of communication whose richness is in proportion to its openness, of *the minimum of order compatible with the maximum of disorder*" (p. 133)), it would seem that Butor has a long way to go yet!

But public intervention is not used merely to satisfy the authors' scruples about chance. Pousseur in particular is concerned with the relationship normally prevailing between composer, performer, and public, which he designates in predominantly Marxist terms as a "master-slave relationship" (*Cahiers*, p. 19), the composer being the master. The alternative, also proposed in Marxist terms, is based on Pousseur's discovery, after he had begun *Votre Faust*, of the book by the philosopher and friend of Brecht, Ernst Bloch, entitled *Das Prinzip Hoffnung* (*The Principle of Hope*). Part of this work[44] is a discussion of drama as a moral, didactic spectacle posing social and political problems to be solved by a participating audience. Pousseur extends this idea by stressing that the audience has a responsibility, of which it may best be made aware by being presented with a work in which it has to participate in a completely literal sense, not just mentally, but through the choice of alternative scenes (*Cahiers*, p. 19). Butor's reasons are less political than esthetic: participation by audience, reader, or critic is invited by the "unfinished" work of art, to create a kind of proliferation. But both authors are in agreement that the final effect is transformatory: "Vocal music transforms life," writes Butor,[45] while Pousseur envisages a future golden era of true cooperation and the invention of a new language, all thanks to music (*Cahiers,* p. 43). To what extent *Votre Faust* contributes toward the foundation of Utopia remains to be seen.

It is clearly a technical *tour de force*, applying the theories outlined above with such effect that it has left most critics totally baffled. The authors have taken advantage of "new means of communication" with a vengeance, especially in the creation of the decor, whose great originality is that it is largely composed of sound, the relatively unimportant visual element being supplied by images projected on a series of screens at the back of the stage: "We wanted a work that was a continuum, that is, one in which there is communication between all its elements, and especially continuous communication between everyday speech and instrumental sounds, through all kinds of intermediaries."[46] A wide variety of comments, shouted, spoken, or instrumental, is provided by means of tape recordings, and varied according to the version of the opera performed. Each sound group has twelve elements, the first consisting of fairground cries; the second, snatches of conversation remembered by Henri and a kind of litany of the heroine's physical attractions; and the last, parts of the musical accompaniment to Part I.[47] This can be further complicated if necessary; for example, in the "Puppet Scene," quotations from Monteverdi's *Orfeo,* Gluck's *Orphée,* Mozart's *Don Giovanni,* and Wagner's *Tristan* are also introduced.

In fact, the "continuum" idea is so widely applied that it is difficult to separate decor from actual drama: everything is quotation. Various poets are used to create a kind of counterpoint with the actual dialogues, including Nerval (his translation of Goethe's *Faust*), Goethe, Marlowe (*Doctor Faustus*), Petrarch, and Góngora. To these must be added quotations in Latin, notably an invocation to the infernal spirits (taken from Marlowe) at the end of Part I. In all, six languages are sung or spoken. The number of composers whose works are quoted from or alluded to is practically endless: those already mentioned, plus Beethoven, Schubert, Mussorgsky, Stravinsky, Webern, Bartok, and Berg. They are distributed, along with the poets, so as to give what the authors call a "color" to the different scenes and variants, which are also literally colored: blue for the room, green for the "cabaret de l'Eglise" (Church tavern), yellow for the street, red for the fair, violet for the port. The "Puppet Scene," for which there are so far four versions, provides a good illustration of this mingling of visual, spoken, and musical decor. Each version is concentrated on a different dais, with a different principal and musicians (who are permanently on stage); in one version, the ballad of the king of Thulé provides a Germanic flavor; in another, long extracts from *Doctor Faustus* create an English atmosphere; in the third, the "Hell scene" from Gluck's *Orphée* provides the French coloring; in the last, parts of da Ponte's libretto for Mozart's *Don Giovanni* (one of the many hints in *Votre Faust* that few if any myths are complete in themselves) are supposed to create an Italian mood. Needless to say, this is only an outline, which cannot do justice to the careful thought that has gone into every detail of the work, whose effects have been very finely calculated.[48]

Yet it is very unlikely that the audience's reaction will depend on the tone or "color" of each scene, as opposed to the actual plot. Indeed, on the only occasion when it is invited to vote—as opposed to intervening spontaneously—the question is: "Will Henri go to the puppet-show with Maggy, or with another woman?" (Finale of Part I). We must therefore decide whether the action is worthy of its intervention.

In its broad lines, the "plot" of *Votre Faust* derives from the major elements of the Faust theme. In the "Prologue on the stage," M. Henri, a composer (alias Faust) is introduced by the impresario (Mephistopheles) to the public, to whom he delivers a talk on serialist music. Afterward, the impresario asks Henri to compose him an opera, with unlimited freedom of resources and treatment, provided it is a *Faust*. Henri agrees but is rapidly distracted from his project by a barmaid called Maggy, who works at an establishment called the "Church tavern" (!) The disapproving impresario uses all means, including blackmail and—in one version—the framing of Maggy with the aid of a pimp, in order to separate them and replace Maggy by a female spy called "the cantatrice." In one version, Maggy dies, and Henri transfers his attentions to her sister who is called, unsurprisingly, Greta (or, in another version, to the "cantatrice"). Most of these events are confined to the first two of the opera's three sections. In section three (actually "deuxième partie, suite" ["part two: continuation"]), Henri and, variously, Greta, Maggy, and the "cantatrice," are pursued by the impresario in a series of very un-Faustian conveyances: a train, a luxury liner, and an airplane. The opera has a variety of endings, although in none of them does Henri get around to writing his *Faust;* in one version (Gallimard, "deuxième partie, suite" ["part two: continuation"]), it is really the impresario who rejects the pact, having finally tired of Henri's procrastination and found another composer; in another (Gallimard, "une autre version de la fin" ["another version of the ending"]), the "cantatrice," using emotional blackmail (she hints at the possibility of a kind of posthumous reconciliation with Maggy), persuades Henri to reject the pact; in another (*L'VII*), Henri and Maggy are reconciled after the framing, and she urges him to reject the pact, which he does this time in the "Finale and epilogue."

If the plot sounds a bit thin, the motivation and dialogue are consistently on the intellectual level of a comic strip. To give only one instance: in the *L'VII* version, the impresario arranges a scene, to be witnessed by Henri, in which it appears that the pimp and

Maggy have been carrying on a love affair during his absence. Henri reacts according to plan, declaring to the impresario: "I'll never leave you again." Yet as soon as Maggy asks to be alone with Henri, the impresario agrees, and in a trice she is able to explain what has happened and urge him to break his agreement. All this, we have seen, has been taken extremely seriously by critics, who complain of the gap between virtuosity of technique and mediocrity of libretto. The chief reason for the unsatisfactory nature of *Votre Faust* does indeed lie here, but it would be an injustice to the authors if we took the plot at all seriously.

For *Votre Faust* is a work depending almost wholly on pastiche and parody. As far as the music is concerned, it is a pastiche in the sense of "a musical composition made up of pieces from different sources" (shorter O.E.D.), and the same applies to the visual and sound decor. As for the text, Butor himself has explained that "the whole text, from the beginning, is a parody" (*Cahiers*, p. 30). So is the title, with its reminiscence of Valéry's "Mon Faust" ["My Faust"], while the word "fantaisie" in the subtitle should also predispose us to treat the work with not too much seriousness. However, there is yet another aspect of parody, which is the product of the authors' subtlety, but has unfortunately backfired. The impresario frequently shows his utter contempt for the business of writing a libretto:

THE IMPRESARIO: Oh yes, the libretto ... [*sic*] Don't bother about that. I'll find that for you. Have you got any particular writer in mind? No, so much the better! Nothing's more dangerous for a musician or a painter than to get interested in literature. It's true that an opera libretto ... [*sic*] What matters is the music.[49]

This view is of course anathema to Butor and Pousseur, to whom all aspects of opera are of equal importance, and closely related. In the complex relation between art and reality in *Votre Faust*, where the fictional Henri never gets around to writing his opera because of the "master-slave relationship" between him and the impresario,[50] the poor quality of the libretto should, I think, be taken as a parodic reflection of the latter's views. There is one very good precedent for this kind of treatment of subject matter: the narrative technique of *Degrés,* whose drabness translates the drabness of what is being taught.

But the authors have committed the mistake of wanting to have their operatic cake and eat it too. On the one hand, *Votre Faust* is a work of the deepest seriousness, an application of Butor and Pousseur's beliefs on a range of very important esthetic and social questions, from the relation between music and drama to the problem of chance in art, the didactic function of opera, and the rôle of collaboration. Above all, most of these questions take on their full meaning in the context of the "open" work. At the same time, the action is apparently to be treated as a parody. If it is not, it is a disgrace. But whichever of these views is correct, the audience is continually called upon to exercise its responsibilities and vote or intervene in order to change the opera's course. Whether the plot is to be treated with seriousness or not, the whole point of the vote—and the supposed responsibility—is therefore lost. Because of this unhappy alliance of triviality and seriousness, *Votre Faust* is unlikely to transform anyone—or anything—until the action is drastically revised. If Lonchampt and Fleuret are to be believed, a good deal of the music is of a high technical standard, but taken as a whole, the work must be classed as an interesting failure, and a sad one after some nine years' collaboration. The authors' virtuosity and desire for a total coverage of their field has undoubtedly led to confusion, and their cerebrality to a lack of contact with the audience. A work whose main aim is to involve has almost certainly had the opposite effect.

CHAPTER 8

Toward the "œuvre ouverte"—*II*

I *Variations on Themes*

SINCE late 1969, when this study was originally begun, Butor has produced his longest work so far, *Oǔ*,[1] essay-poems on Fourier (nautically entitled *La Rose des vents*)[2] and Beethoven (*Dialogue avec 33 variations de Ludwig van Beethoven sur une valse de Diabelli*),[3] and numerous critical essays. As I write (April, 1972), *Travaux d'approche* has just appeared in the Gallimard "poésie" collection.[4] Butor has also found time to visit Australia and New Zealand in addition to his year at the University of New Mexico, and does some teaching at the University of Nice, preparation for which takes him at least two days a week. He has also moved house twice, a process which must have made the "library-prison" seem very much a reality . . .[5]

To use an analogy that might please Butor, *Oǔ*, the Fourier, and the Beethoven could be likened to various aspects of a musical work, possibly three movements of a concerto, linked by certain common themes, yet separable by virtue of their treatment of them. The first, basically *largo*, is paradoxically the easiest of access yet the hardest to interpret, and appears pessimistic in its first-person presentation of Butor's descriptive battle with the Sandia Mountains. The second is even more difficult to categorize, since Fourier's strange mixture of crackpot seriousness, inspired prophesying, and humor[6] carries over into Butor's extrapolations: one is left in doubt how to take such a farrago. Finally, the Beethoven is a credit to Butor's culture and imagination, a test of the reader's, and yet an obviously, even naïvely Utopian work which reminds one of the pieces on Monet or Rothko in its determination to present the artist as a contestor of the established order and an anticipator of the future order of things.

II *Two Aspects of Utopia*

In 1940, André Breton made his first acquaintance with Fourier's works during a stay in America, reading them while visiting the Hopi Indians.[7] The revelation was profound—it must frequently have seemed as if he were reading himself—and resulted in the *Ode à Charles Fourier*, first published in 1947.[8] In its turn, *La Rose des vents* is dedicated to Breton—and Roland Barthes, whose own essay on Fourier first appeared shortly after Butor's in 1970.[9] For Butor, as for Breton, Fourier seems to have acted primarily as a confirmer of thoughts and an already established literary practice, as a stimulating perspective from an unusual source; at all events, his name should be added to those of Mallarmé, Breton, and Umberto Eco whenever one wishes to delimit the intellectual and poetic context within which Butor works.

La Rose des vents is in many respects a work for initiates (of Butor and Fourier); to the noninitiate, it must read like an amusing fantasy on—possibly even parody of—Fourier's preposterously imaginative social and cosmological system. The first nine of its thirty-two sections are basically a review of the nine phases of humanity's progress actually described by Fourier, together with references to various aspects of his work such as the rôle of analogy, the range of passions, the new species or "contre-moules" that will one day inhabit the earth ("antilions," "antileopards," etc.), even the famous transformation of the seas into lemonade. Butor then continues the series, keeping within the framework of Fourier's mathematics, his vocabulary (e.g., p. 119: "Foyer ultérieur principal/ 21 INTERPAUSE: Herschel l'archifé" ['Principal subsequent pivot/ 21 INTERPAUSE: Herschel the arch-fairy"]), his social psychology, and his cosmology, but attempting to develop the widest-ranging—and often the most humorous—consequences. *La Rose* contains some hilarious passages, not all of them from Fourier's pen. The spectacle of the whole of humanity as "voyeurs" (p. 119), the description of the interplanetary exchange of erotic letters (p. 112), or the reign of the "bearded lady omniarch" (p. 93) are worthy of Fourier at his most playful. That *La Rose* is at times amusing, and always ingenious, does not, however, preclude boredom, even in the initiate; pages of complicated[10] extrapolations from Fourier's own conveniently ambiguous[11] calculations (e.g. *Rose*, pp. 151–57) make tedious reading, and one is tempted to jump whole sections. The reader without a detailed knowledge of both Fourier and Butor is likely to abandon ship very quickly.

If one has this knowledge, the work, and the fact of its existence, assume great importance. Fourier's three great innovations (they are of course linked) are in the broad realms of social psychology, language, and mathematics. The first, the theory of "l'attraction passionnée" (lit., "passionate attraction"), is an attempt to cater to all men's passions and desires, from the so-called normal to the extremes of what is still regarded as sexual perversion, by arranging for their continual satisfaction within the context of a new, harmonious society. In the Utopia of social relationships love becomes "the pivot of society."[12] This aspect of Fourier's thought greatly appealed to Breton and the Surrealists, although Butor's treatment of it in *La Rose* tends to emphasize such amusingly erotic illustrations as the "gratte-talons," the man who satisfied his desires by scratching his mistress's feet (pp. 114–15); in short, it is not of vital importance to him.

The two other innovations are, however, crucial in the light of Butor's formal experimentation, although to see any startling coincidence between Fourier's use of analogy and Butor's poetic procedures to date would be a mistake—in spite of the former's undoubted influence on Surrealist poetry.[13] The Fouriériste analogy is always precise, leaving no scope for ambiguity, and invariably explained, whereas Butor's poetry is essentially a "trying out" by juxtaposition, relying on alliteration and encounter.[14] But Fourier's experiments with the architecture of his books, his refusal to be bound by traditional criteria of textual order, and his desire to achieve absolute congruence of theme and form anticipate Butor's own experimentation in the "mobile" works to a remarkable degree. The theory of "series" should surely be presented in a serial manner: hence the initially bewildering architecture of the *Traité de l'association domestique agricole* (later *Théorie de l'unité universelle*), which is no more than a practical application of his theories: "Foreword, Introduction, Counter-pivot, Prolegomena, Direct pivot," etc.[15] Commenting on this, René Schérer writes: "It is a 'montage,' a 'collage' governed by a secret logic. . . . This 'unreadable' book is, by virtue of its form, the first act of a literary revolution unfortunately without results.[16] "Without results?" The rest of the description would fit *Mobile* exactly.

Finally, Fourier's concept of the "series," which enables him to calculate, to the minutest degree, everything from the ideal size of the "phalange" to the development and decline of humanity, not to mention the future evolution of the universe, provides a reasonably close corroboration of Butor's theory and practice of the "open" work. For Fourier, the series (O.E.D. "Series II. I. *Math.* A set of terms in succession, finite or infinite in number, the value of each of which is determined by its ordinal position according to a definite rule known as the *law* of the series.") is frequently based on 7 (the musical octave: musical comparisons and illustrations abound in his writings), 3, 4, or 12, and its great advantage over a purely additive system, as Simone Debout has brilliantly explained, is that it accounts for development: it is *dynamic* in conception:

> By means of the series one can link all things in the course of development, things situated between a "before" and an "after"; the series account for the cohesion of distinct or even divergent elements, but also for the cohesion of things within time, of the past and the future. They are, writes Fourier, "living mathematics," that is to say that measurement is no longer fixed in an eternal calm, but the movement of life carries the law itself along in its dynamism.[17]

For the theorician of the "livre futur," what would appeal most about the series would be the link it provides between past, present, and future; as he puts it when discussing Fourier's cosmology: "The development of *trans-mundane* genealogy makes possible the organization of the present in the light of the knowledge of the past, but also the prediction of the future" (*Rose*, p. 132). As this study has repeatedly emphasized, the fundamental task for Butor is to organize material whose main characteristic is that it is neither "stationary" nor isolated, but moving and affected by other elements—in short, a universe of fluctuating relations which seems reasonably close to the one described by modern science. In consequence, he has evolved the "mobile" work, in a threefold attempt to be faithful to that universe: descriptively, poetically (the use of juxtaposition), and didactically: the variable structures of the text invite participation by the reader and hence a proliferation of interpretations and, eventually, future texts.

This basically dynamic approach to reality and its transmutation into literature, the optimism inherent in the constant appeal to the future, and Butor's long-standing fascination with mathematics, clearly make him receptive to Fourier's ideas. The series encourages expansion while providing a structure for it, points to the future while paying due attention to the past, and, in conjunction with analogy, reconciles diversity with totality. But as far as I can see it does not—cannot—allow for indetermination, that area of chance inherent in the theories which surround aleatory music, and particularly in those of Umberto Eco and Henri Pousseur. In failing to do so, it might be seen to restrict the freedom—and responsibility—with which Butor and Pousseur are both so concerned. On the other hand, the superabundance of material within a serial and therefore extensible framework could be seen as equivalent to Pousseur's notion of "surdétermination" [overdetermination], which he resorts to in order to resolve the determination/indetermination problem.[18]

Fourier's illustration of his theories is of course *incomplete*—only nine of the thirty-two periods of humanity are actually described—and as such provides an ideal starting point for Butor, as he acknowledges: "Truth can only come about through the action of a very carefully constructed but fragmentary work, of a counter-ruin, one that has even been falsified . . ." (*Rose,* p. 14). On the contrary, the Diabelli variations are more than complete in the sense that, as far as one knows, Beethoven had no intention of writing more than 33: in fact, he was only asked for one by the publisher-composer. But it is characteristic of Butor that Beethoven's expansion of one into thirty-three should be seen as a starting point only and that he should suggest still further proliferation. It is also characteristic that the variations should be seen as "an autobiography and an indispensable means of enabling us to enjoy the view that Beethoven could have had of his sonatas, and of the whole of his work" (*Dialogue,* p. 137). The *Dialogue* also takes up one of the themes of *Votre Faust,* the unhappy relationship between composer and publisher or impresario, claiming among other things that "the aim was to make the theme [of Diabelli] criticize itself, to extract from the lamentable situation of contemporary music in relation to the god-publisher, the possibility of a new form of music and of life" (p. 65).[19]

But the most extraordinary features of the *Dialogue* are its own organization, based, like that of *La Rose,* on Fourier's principles, and its application of those principles to Beethoven. According to Butor, Henri Pousseur was the first to point out the importance of the number 32 in Beethoven's later works: the 32 variations in C minor without opus number, the 32 sonatas, and the 33 variations ("that is, 32 plus an introduction, the theme, and a finale, the minuet with variations," p. 36). A "pivot" is thus supposedly formed by the sixteenth to seventeenth variations, the second one beginning by reversing the opening of the first (p. 33), the variations are analyzed in terms of various "versants"—"terrestrial," "patient," "celestial," "future," and so on.

Butor's main purpose in all this is to demonstrate that the Diabelli variations are a commentary on the history of music and its present state,[20] and an evocation of the future; the three phases are of course linked: "If certain [variations] of the second [versant] point toward musicians of the past, it is only insofar as they are pregnant with the future, capable of instruction, of unexpected developments, and this is why for us they also point toward future composers" (p. 138). The essential point here is that, for Butor, the future and expansion are synonymous. The variations are first scrutinized for a possible "gap," a means of widening the work as it stands. This he finds at the "pivot" (p. 34). Next, Butor suggests that the variations by other contributors (among them, Schubert) be added at the beginning of Beethoven's 33 (pp. 70–71); finally, Beethoven's dream of this Mozartian successor (according to Butor, p. 140), provokes a Butorian one: "It is as if the expanded performance suggested to us by the text could not only be preceded by a first circle composed of variations chosen from the second Diabelli album, but also invited another spiral, even vaster, interminable, formed by the contribution of future musicians" (p. 141).

In turn, it is not particularly difficult to imagine what a professional musicologist would make of all this, although I have yet to read an analysis of the *Dialogue* by one. As far as I can judge, without proper musical competence, Butor's justification of the key structural rôle of variations 16–17 is sound. But the general application of Fourier to an analysis of Beethoven still seems arbitrary, and the detailed commentary is frequently no more than pleasant fantasy[21]—acceptable as such, but hardly convincing as contributory argument. The *Dialogue* is also devoid of the humor of the *Rose*, but only slightly less fastidious; in short, there are few compensations for the nonspecialist reader, and probably irritation for the expert. I would rate it among the least attractive and least convincing books that Butor has written.

III *The Agony of Writing*

Its length apart, *Où* is in some ways a respite after the rigorous fantasies of the Beethoven and the Fourier, with the "old" Butor manifesting himself in various ways. The work bears a strong resemblance to *Mobile* or *6 810 000 Litres*, with juxtaposition of themes and "tainting" by contiguity, use of indentation, roman and italic, integration of secondary material, and progression from simplicity—and banality—to complication and poetry. Many familiar subjects reappear within the predominantly American setting: travel by automobile, violence, religious bigotry, the fate of the Negro, the climate, and colors. On the other hand, comparison with the first volume of *Le Génie du lieu* reveals the extent of Butor's development since 1958, not only in form, but in depth and breadth of thematic conception.

The title is intriguing: *Où* ("where," "the place where," or "when": all noninterrogative), with the accent crossed out to give *Ou* ("or": a series of alternatives) and hence implying temporal and spatial alternatives, a criss-crossing of memories and descriptions of various places, which the shape of the "x" also suggests. The text consists of nine overlapping parts, according to the index, or eight if one considers the two pieces on Paris as different aspects of a single poem. In either case a convenient link with Fourier could be established, the more so as the work's general arithmetic seems to be based on odd numbers, with *seven* the most important.[22] The parts, in order of their first appearance, are: "I've fled Paris"; "35 Views of Mt. Sandia on winter evenings";[23] "The Mud at Seoul"; "Nine other Views of Mt. Sandia"; "The Rain at Angkor"; "The Fog at Santa Barbara"; "I hate Paris"; "The Snow between Bloomfield and Bernalillo"; "The Cold at Zuni." Most could be subheaded "The hazards of tourism": Butor abandoned in the rain at Angkor-Wat, nearly bogged down in snow after a conference, freezing on an Indian reserve, or startled by a bomb in a faculty club. All are formed by the interrelation of elements, ranging from different time layers (e.g., in "The Rain at Angkor") to the obsessive intrusion of previous material from the same section— and foreign material from others—in the Sandia pieces. Secondary material is used extensively: the description of the "Shalako" ceremonies is traversed by Butor's own adaptation of two native chants,[24] while the visit to Brigham Young University is a veritable *collage*, with an amusing genesis and implications.

The department of French at Brigham Young has the most complete collection of Marcel Schwob documents in the world, including "the pearl, the priceless pearl,"[25] the only surviving letter of his mistress, who inspired Schwob's insipid *Livre de Monelle*. This book is utilized by Butor in a variety of ways. The heroine's love of snow and her evocation of a "realm of white," the narrator's habitation of a "realm of black" and his desire for a "realm of red,"[26] give Butor three colors: white (the snow during part of the return journey), black (the darkness of part of the return journey), and red (violence: the history of the Mormons as related in *The Book of Mormon* and by Apollinaire). Monelle, Schwob's "salutary prostitute," is contrasted ironically with examples of the Mormons' absurd puritanism and also forms part of a series of young women who figure in *Où:* girls desired in the metro in "I hate Paris," or foreign *émigrées* who furnish fresh breeding material for the Mormons in Apollinaire's *La Femme assise*.[27] Finally, Monelle's assertion that "everything constructed uses débris, and there is nothing new on earth save forms" (pp. 22–23 not cited) would hardly be lost on the author of *Où*.

The main function of Apollinaire's little-known potboiler, also quoted extensively, is also contrastive and ironic; its heroine, Paméla, is a witness of a scene of brutality—the lynching of a negro by the Mormons (*Où*, pp. 187–92)—the immediacy of which stands out against the stereotyped bloodbaths of the *Book of Mormon* (e.g., *Où*, pp. 157–58).[28] Butor's point here seems to be that violence and puritanism are necessary conditions of each other, a thesis that has a good deal of support from historical fact.

The principle of contrast, which can frequently be observed in the arrangement of the elements forming each section, is in fact the major force governing *Où*. Descriptions of winter (fog, mud, rain, snow, ice) illuminated by the desire for the sun's return, the

transience of the written word, apparently defeated by the permanence of Mount Sandia, liquidity versus solidity, above all absence
(in time and space) versus presence: it is only when *Où* is examined
in the light of these contrasts that the "hazards of tourism" take on
their true significance. With the exception of the poems on Paris,
which are climatically "neutral," the whole of the book is set in
winter and frequently in darkness or semidarkness as well. One of
the characteristics of winter weather is that it constitutes a series
of obstacles hindering the completion of the tourist's "task": the
mud ("fifth element" [*sic*], p. 37) at Seoul almost prevents Butor
from returning from his excursion in time to give a talk (pp. 34–38),
at Angkor-Wat a sudden downpour almost cuts off his return to the
"Auberge Royale" (pp. 54–62), and the snow between Bloomfield and
Bernalillo (pp. 129–256) makes return to Albuquerque seem doubtful.
And while the cold at Zuni is not so much an obstacle as a discomfort,
it is interesting that the one symbolic aspect of the multipurpose[29]
ceremonies stressed by Butor is the perpetuation of the East (pp. 364
and 367) in order that the sun may not die. Meanwhile, the second
series of "descriptions" of Mount Sandia with which the account of
the Shalako is interspersed becomes in part an invocation to the sun
(e.g., IV, p. 333 and VII, p. 365).

These and other episodes can, I think, be treated on two, sometimes
three levels: the first, humorous, one is simply the discomfort put
up with by the indefatigable Butor, spurred on by "le démon du
voyage" as he once put it in a letter: the second is a modern transposition of Heine's "Ein Fichtenbaum steht einsam . . .," the desire
for a state opposite to the one in which one is placed: Butor in
Paris hates it, then flees it, but desires it while away: the absence-
presence theme: the third is a concrete manifestation of the familiar
Butorian theme of "enlisement," sinking in a quicksand, unable to
achieve anything, and an echo of one of his activities while in
Albuquerque—the seemingly vain attempts to describe Mount
Sandia. As one commentator has put it: "The words, not being set
in a phrase, are hurled at it like stones"[30]: the most moving part of
Où is undoubtedly the descriptive battle with the mountain looked
onto by Butor's window. Page after page of "variations on a theme,"
interrupted, taken up again, invaded by other parts of the text,
erased, modified, frustrated by the passing of time and the changing
light, bear witness to the difficulties of writing, in a personal manner

unusual for Butor, who had previously taken refuge in this respect behind a Revel or a Vernier:

At first these whitening pillars of claws that become tentacles I could have used "chalky, pallid, towers, battlements" and the letters breaking off one by one and closing up—after traversing the zone of despondency I try to go on: (etc, p. 19)
At first these clenched fists of strata the word "stumps" and the letters breaking off one by one go on: *imagine falls staffs making firm drying winds stump a net.* (etc., p. 213)
every mountain is indescribable (p. 19 *passim*)
the words I have traced out break up into stony letters (p. 137)
I despair (p. 321)
this isn't at all what I thought I had to say (p. 392: last page of book)

The contrast of elements in *San Marco* has been reversed: the Cathedral/monument, symbol of man's creativity, opposed its stability to the threat of "engulfment" by the lagoon and the babble of visitors; here, Mount Sandia opposes its permanence to the flux of man's descriptive efforts, where even the word "description" is in doubt (e.g., p. 132 *passim*: "my description [is it a description?]"). Similarly, the dance of the Shalako, presented by Butor as the culminating point of the Indian ceremonies (which it is not[31]), is never actually described, although the events of the earlier part of the evening are recounted at interminable length. Time[32]—or textual space—runs out.

What, then, are the conditions for a successful (i.e., poetic) description? According to Hubert Juin, "distance and echoing are the elements necessary for a possible creation of language."[33] It might have been slightly more appropriate to choose "absence" instead of "distance." For just as "I hate Paris, because it prevents me from seeing Paris, from being in Paris, from spreading myself there./ I hate Paris because it bars me from Paris" (pp. 143–44), similarly it is the *presence* of Mount Sandia—the descriptions are in the present tense[34]—that hinders Butor's task. His point seems to be the Proustian one that reality can only be discovered via memory—which implies absence. Whereas the rediscovered past can be experienced as situated "outside" time, the present—as the fragmented views of Mount Sandia show all too clearly—is not really the *instant* sought by Butor,[35] but a *succession* of instants implying change within time.

And yet, what of the descriptions in the past (Seoul, Angkor), the anecdotal banality of which seems to destroy Butor's point? What of the example of Jacques Revel, which implied the tragic futility of pretending that the past is immutable? What of the awareness of the extent—but not the impossibility—of the difficulties implied by "nobody has yet thought of giving names to all that" (p. 64), or the cautious optimism of the repeated "Blind deaf it is years of blindness and deafness from which I am painfully freeing myself" (e.g., p. 221)? One answer to this series of questions would be, I think, an esthetic one, the delicate balance between the tension, flux, and undeniable vitality of the provisional pieces on Mount Sandia, the finished banality of certain other parts of the book in which they appear, and the rigid general framework: far better attempt a poetic description, a revitalization of language, perhaps doomed to failure, than toss off a few pages of travel souvenirs; far better allow the reader room for completion and reorganization than present him with ready-made pieces, which the Seoul and Angkor episodes are to a large extent. Another answer would again use the word "balance": Butor is incapable of writing a pessimistic book, and there have been times when his optimism is rather difficult to accept. In *Où*, the balance between the expression of the difficulty of writing and the optimism inherent in the fact that an *unfinished* description is both a celebration of potentiality[36] and an invitation to completion, is admirably kept. *Où* is one of the richest of Butor's "open" works, and a useful corrective to the sometimes naïve enthusiasm of the Fourier and the Beethoven.

IV   *Surrealism and Butor's Poetic Practice*

In recent years, Butor has turned more and more to poetry, after a period in the 1950's and early 1960's, when he appears to have written virtually none. As a poet, and in general literary terms, he is both derivative and original; in the words of Paul Valéry: "The lion is made of digested sheep"[37]— Butor's originality precludes neither his direct or indirect debt to many earlier writers nor the numerous affinities between him and his contemporaries, in France and elsewhere. Where direct influence is involved, I have already suggested in Chapter 1 that it comes from two sources, both of which are primarily poetic. But whereas the influence of

Mallarmé is now generally acknowledged by critics and has been examined in some detail by one,[38] the many similarities between Butor and the Surrealists are only just beginning to be uncovered.[39] References to Surrealism and its exponents in his writings are not particularly frequent, although one or two have been noted in the course of this study. More indicative of his interest are essays on Raymond Roussel, Michel Leiris, and André Breton, all of which show a detailed knowledge of their works and an undisguised admiration.[40] Butor has also written a short piece on Surrealist painting for a Parisian medical trade journal, the most unlikely outlet for his work that he has so far used.[41] Some of the Surrealists' interests are also Butor's, as an early article on "L'Alchimie et son langage"[42] and his fascination by the writings of Charles Fourier testify. Another highly original article is entitled "Le Point suprême et l'âge d'or à travers quelques œuvres de Jules Verne" ("The Supreme Point and the Golden Age as seen in some works of Jules Verne")—an obvious reference to two fundamental and closely related tenets of literary Surrealism; in it, Butor discusses the search for the North Pole in *Les Aventures du capitaine Hatteras* in the light of a passage from Breton's *Second Manifeste du Surréalisme*. As Hatteras approaches the Pole, an atmosphere of purity and calm surrounds his vessel, which is bathed in a kind of luminous darkness. "Isn't this luminous night the solution to all antinomies? It's obvious: the Pole clearly signifies that central point mentioned by Breton, the point at which night and day, sea and sky cease to appear contradictory," comments Butor.[43]

The search for Paradise Lost or the struggle to found Utopia is thus the first preoccupation common to Butor and the Surrealists; his essays on Rousseau and Montaigne,[44] which interpret their work similarly to Jules Verne's, or theoretical pieces such as "Le Roman et la poésie,"[45] have their counterparts in the writings of Breton in particular, whose Utopianism is most fervently expressed in his *Ode à Charles Fourier*.[46] Jean Gaulmier, in his edition of the *Ode*, draws numerous parallels between the propositions of Fourier and Breton, particularly the "conviction ... that Desire and Love, the only divine impulses in a world transcended by no Divine Being, guide man toward the magic point where all contradictions are resolved in the white incandescence of Uniteism[sic]"[47] As we have seen, it is Butor's faith in the power of language rather than Love and Desire that underlies his conviction that Utopia will one day be attained. In this respect, however, his utopianism is merely less broadly based than that of the Surrealists, who attach similar importance to language, but as a contributory reason for hope.

The second parallel is mainly in the domain of the novel, where Butor and Breton use dreams and an apparatus of coincidence, symbolism, and mythology to indicate that personal or material "reality" is only a thin veil hiding an infinitely richer and more significant order of existence. Although the latter detested realism in the novel and vowed to destroy it, a statement in his *Le Surréalisme et la peinture* reveals a more moderate attitude toward *reality*: "Everything I love, everything I think and feel, inclines me toward a special philosophy of immanence according to which surreality is contained within reality itself, and is neither above nor outside it.[48] In every novel except *Degrés*, Butor gradually reveals that surface reality is the smallest—but still useful—part of a rigid, esoteric construct involving symbol, myth, coincidence, "signs," dreams, and hallucination. *L'Emploi du temps* in particular reads at times like a demonstration of the principle of "hasard objectif" ("objective chance"), with signs and coincidence governing its hero's acts; in the words of Breton, "there are facts which . . . each time present all the appearances of a signal . . . which mean that when quite alone I discover improbable complicities which convince me of my illusion each time I believe that I am alone at the helm of the ship."[49] In a more general sense, the infinite care with which Butor bestows mythical or symbolic significance on the tiniest detail of his novels, from their title to numerous apparently trivial acts within them, is a practical application of his belief that "the world, both in its totality and in its detail, is a cipher."[50] The dosage varies, of course, as does the subtlety with which the underlying layers are revealed; on the whole, Butor is not particularly concerned with concealing the complication and mystery of his novelistic universe from the reader, and allows him plenty of clues. Nevertheless, so close is the interrelation of the various elements that only the patient researches of some commentators have been able to uncover the richness of Butor's material. The "mobile" texts are perhaps less rewarding in this respect, although *Mobile* and *Réseau aérien* make considerable use of dreams and hallucination.

Finally, Butor and Breton emphasize the social rôle of the writer, not as a creator of "littérature engagée" but as a manipulator of language. In a famous passage from the *Second Manifeste du Surréalisme*, Breton writes:

> The problem of social action—I return to this point and insist on it—is only one aspect of a more general problem which Surrealism has made it its duty to raise and which is *the problem of human expression in all its forms.* By expression one means, at the outset, language. One must therefore not be surprised to see Surrealism operating from the very outset almost solely on the level of language ....[51]

Language must be rejuvenated, given a new vitality, in order that we may develop our imaginative potential. This key point is developed by Breton and Butor in various theoretical writings,[52] and although their practice might seem to differ, with the former indulging in automatic writing, in fact there is considerable similarity between Breton's use of contrasting images and Butor's fondness for juxtaposition.

It is here that I must express some reservations about Butor's use of language, for in spite of the rigid architecture of his works, and his insistence on "control" and "form," they are not exempt from a poetic diffuseness. The influence of certain quasi-Surrealists, notably Raymond Roussel, may be partly responsible. Quite a cult has been growing around the author of *Comment j'ai écrit certains de mes Livres* in recent years: as well as Butor, André Breton, Jean Ricardou, Alain Robbe-Grillet, Michel Foucault, Michel Leiris, and Bernard Caburet have all written enthusiastically on him since 1950. Roussel's word games and fertile imagination produce at best a series of amusingly preposterous, intriguing, but gratuitous tableaux, at worst sheer incoherence, illustrating the point at which the greatest quality of Surrealism turns into its most serious liability, when our experience has been so broadened that it vanishes into nothingness. The full development of language and of our imagination is a laudable enterprise, but it is doubtful whether the kind of Rousselian assault, in which our sensibility is battered by incongruities, is the best way of achieving this end. As a prelude to my reservations about Butor's use of language, I can do no better than quote one of the best theorists on current cultural trends, Leonard B. Meyer:

> ... it is by no means self-evident that a broadening of categorical sensibility is per se valuable, particularly if it is achieved at the expense of nuance

and refinement of perception and response. And it is not unreasonable to suppose that a succession of radical innovations tends to preclude subtle and precise understanding. What is gained in breadth may well be lost in depth.[53]

Two of Butor's earliest poetic texts, which have only recently been published ("La Banlieue de l'aube à l'aurore" and "Mouvement brownien"),[54] betray a transparent debt to literary Surrealism in their use of contrasting images:

> La mer est un fruit sans noyaux
> Les hirondelles broutent le ciel cru
> Au loin les automobiles chantent
> La pluie se promène avec des bas de soie
>
> Les chameaux dans le ciel
> Chavirent avec mélancolie (. . .) ("La Banlieue . . .")[55]

> [The sea is a fruit without stones
> The swallows munch the raw sky
> Far off the automobiles sing
> The rain walks in silken stockings
>
> The camels in the sky
> Capsize in melancholy fashion (. . .)]

They also employ cumulation, which, with the powerful contrasts, creates an effect which is present in many of his later poems, a kind of luxuriant lethargy indicating, in its turn, nostalgia and disorientation:

> Les sucres d'orge sont décidément moins bons
> Les billes d'agate se font rares
> La tour Eiffel penche la tête
> Avec un sourire mil neuf cent
> Manche à gigot panier à salade crise de nerfs
> On tombe à pic ("La Banlieue")

> [The barley sugars are definitely less good
> The agate drops are hard to find
> The Eiffel Tower bends its head
> With a 1900 smile
> Leg-of-mutton holder salad basket [or "police van"] attack of nerves
> We're just in time]

"La Banlieue" and "Mouvement brownien" are illustrated by
Bernard Dufour, whereas in other pieces the process is reversed and
Butor himself "illustrates," in writing, the subjects of photographs,
paintings, or engravings—which are often not reproduced as an
accompaniment to his text. In short, the "subject" of the "illustration" is often absent. Through this "illustration," he is able to
indulge his interest in plastic art and express his feelings through
the choice of an artist with whom he has an emotional affinity;
a poem like *Dialogues des règnes*[56] indicates how "illustration"
turns into poetic creation in its repetition of "fog," "darkness,"
"sleep," and in the dominant theme of exile and disorientation.
It is also an excellent example of Butor's imaginative—and mathematical—power, which is richly inventive of frequently exotic
imagery, and its efficacy is far from being on an intellectual level.
This is, of course, scarcely surprising, since the main function of
poetry has always been beyond the realm of the intellect, especially
so since the late nineteenth century; at the same time, the precision
and density of a Rimbaud seem preferable to the games of a Roussel.
In Butor's case, it is a failure to restrain the flow, to limit the
cumulation, to sacrifice some alliteration and assonance in favor
of a more varied and concise form, above all to temper the desire
to liberate our imagination by a willingness to satisfy our reason too,
that prevents me from submitting completely to the undeniable
power of his language—in his poetry or other literary forms. Butor
is indeed, in the words of Alain Bosquet, a "baroque lyrical poet,"[57]
and I am not convinced that his preciosity is invariably an asset.

Basically, however, what I—or others—have on occasion named
"preciosity" stems from something else, a concept of poetry which
has developed over the years from Butor's Surrealistic beginnings:
the placing in apposition of words or clusters of words, as described
in Chapter 1.[58] In the Preface-cum-interview to a recent volume
of poems, *Travaux d'Approche*, Butor discusses this process in
connection with his more recent practice of self-quotation, or a
reworking of previously published pieces:

Instead of being definitively fixed (sometimes admirably fixed as in an
inscription), words can attain a superior state of being in which they
perpetually awaken other words. Something trembles in them. This is
what the title "Mouvement brownien" attempted to evoke.

If a person reworks a text, it is because when he reread it, he felt that the   -
words weren't at rest, that some mutually excluded each other, demanded

to change place, to disappear, that others on the contrary called for commentaries and complements. After a certain number of "versions" (a very apt and fine term because it designates something which turns: the turning of pages within the book), the text becomes fixed, solidifies. It is at the precise moment when I can no longer make it move that I publish it. (p. 17)

In other words, there is a proliferation *within* his work, just as Butor hopes that, when finally published, the text itself will engender a proliferation of others. Put another way still, the process is an *exhaustive* one, where the only limiting factor, economically speaking, is the mathematical framework within which the words, hopefully, develop their potentiality.

But in concrete terms—what appears on the page—the results seem to me to be frequently disappointing; once the dominant theme or tone has been identified, the variations on it spin on endlessly, often producing little more than a jumble of sounds. Butor seems to recognize the danger of this in *Où*, where the problem of "which alternative is most appropriate" is raised in the Sandia pieces. But elsewhere it seems as if *all* alternatives are equally valid. Consequently a poem like *Dialogues des règnes* or *Litanie d'eau*[59] rapidly loses its effectiveness, its imagery overwhelming and then wearying the reader in a manner reminiscent of Victor Hugo, although Butor's technique is very different.[60] In the latter poem, ten engravings of successive seascapes by Gregory Masurovsky are reproduced in the first published version. Its impact is considerably reduced in the later, Gallimard form, although not because the engravings are omitted, which is Butor's usual practice. The real reason is that the original disposition of the words on the page emphasized the text's rhythmic qualities:

Va grise   revient   s'étale   grise vague enfle roule
chevelure gris d'argent   va vient lame grise   revient
sous le soleil d'eau   s'étend   s'étale eau douce   grise
pétales de la claire mer   l'horizon gris   le soleil d'argent
le ciel s'allonge   flamme grise   monte montagne blanche   roule
croule va   s'aplanit soie grise   vient   respire velours gris

[Goes gray   returns   unfolds   gray wave swells rolls
gray hair of silver   goes comes gray wave   returns
beneath the sun of water   stretches out   unfolds soft water   gray
petals of the clear sea   the gray horizon   the sun of silver
the sky lengthens   gray flame   mounts white mountain   rolls
collapses goes   flattens out gray silk   comes   breathes velvet   gray]

Ten pages of this would be impressive, the rhythm and repetitions
(the whole is of course minutely structured) creating a sense of
movement and instability consonant with the subject matter; the
eighty of the Gallimard version are quite excessive. *Common Shirley*,
a piece illustrating eight engravings of a nude woman by the same
artist, utilizes the same techniques (minus the spacing), but allied to
a concision and humor which to me are poetically more successful:

> Mousseuse comme un torrent,
> généreusement je m'étends, je me répands,
> marine houleusement, je m'éclaircis
> comme une plage immensément je me détends,
> prairie, fougère, onduleuse,
> miséricordieusement cygne
> je me fonds écumeuse,
> nacrée, je me déroule,
> m'enneige.[61]

> [Frothing as a torrent,
> I stretch out generously, spread out,
> sea-like swellingly, I lighten,
> like a beach immensely I relax,
> meadow, fern, sinuous,
> mercifully swan
> I melt foaming,
> nacreous, I unfold,
> as snow.]

Paradoxically, it is the novels—with the exception of *Degrés*—and
the "mobile" pieces which seem to me to be poetically more
successful than the poetry published as such. The manipulation of
"elemental" imagery (fire, water, sun, etc.), the changes rung on the
simplest of words,[62] the reworking of myth and use of dreams,
create a text in which economy of structure and precision of language
are allied. Just occasionally I feel that Butor is not completely in
control, as he himself admits in the case of *Passage de Milan*, while
there is a kind of baroque exuberance in *L'Emploi du temps*, where
certain passages[63] are difficult to justify in terms of their thematic
relevance. In short, in all domains of his work, Butor has been
rather too prodigal with his poetic gifts, when slightly more discretion in their application would have enriched his readers'
sensibility without confusing it.

CHAPTER 9

Conclusion

I *Butor and the "nouveau roman"*

THE affinities between Butor and other exponents of the "nouveau roman" have been examined by many critics, and I have
no intention of repeating at length what has already been very well
said,[1] especially as to describe him as a novelist is to ignore everything he has written since 1960, and a good deal before. Butor's
novels, like those of Robbe-Grillet, Nathalie Sarraute, or Claude
Simon, are essentially a "mise en question" of a complicated and
unstable world, owing a good deal to the descriptive philosophy
of phenomenology. In the course of this questioning, most of the
features of the traditional novel are discarded. Chronological
narration of events is usually replaced by the protagonist's experience
of time as something which is inevitably flexible and discontinuous,
with past, present, and future alternating without any comforting
pattern. The protagonist himself is no longer fixed, "rounded," or
interesting in himself: it is not the anonymous photoelectric cell-
narrator of Robbe-Grillet's *La Jalousie* who fascinates, but we are
intrigued by the way in which "his" vision deforms certain objects
"he" perceives. Nor does the protagonist hold very interesting
conversations with his friends; instead, he usually reflects or reminisces mentally about his confusing experiences in a kind of interior
monologue, the essence of which is the unavailability to him of a
coherently organized body of knowledge. Sometimes the writer
appears hardly less confused than his hero; at all events, the self-
reflecting or narcissistic novel in which a fictional character is
trying—usually unsuccessfully—to write the same novel as the
author, has been a common phenomenon since the early 1950's.
One very important consequence is that the reader tends to become
involved in the creation of some kind of novel from the unassembled
elements, "fictional" or "real", with which he is confronted.

  These mainly negative characteristics of the "nouveau roman"
have led to charges of useless formalism, which are difficult to

refute completely.[2] Nevertheless, Butor's novels—and his other writings—are largely exempted from such criticisms by many positive features: their didacticism and the exemplary nature of their heroes, their oblique attack on many aspects of Western European society, and especially their attempt to use language as a means of transforming reality. For Butor is not prepared to submit to chaos by describing it, even if the description entails the imposition of a *literary* pattern. The function of literature, he believes, far exceeds its initial task of "catching up with" a world-in-flux; having caught up, it must then describe it in such a way as to act on it: "Thus poetry, critic of life today, undertakes to change it for us."[3] Form is not merely an end in itself, a refuge from committed art, but an (indirect) means of altering our way of life. Literature for Butor has, we have seen, a *social* efficacy; it has primacy over politics, into which he has only made one major excursion. For the root of our misery lies deeper than the particular government or political system under which we live; it is linguistic, the inability of language to keep pace with and then transform reality. Literature is therefore not an end in itself, divorced from or only partially in contact with life, but a means of studying our relation with reality (the phenomenological function) and then provoking change as a prelude to a better and more harmonious future.

II *Butor Today*

Speaking with Madeleine Chapsal in 1960, Sartre claimed that "there is today, in France, someone who has the ambition to become and every chance of becoming a great writer. The first since 1945: Butor."[4] It would be rash, some twelve years later, to confirm or deny this tentative prophecy. Butor is still relatively young and extremely active, and has certainly compelled a greater degree of recognition than the three other major exponents of the new novel, in part because of his achievements in other fields. No other contemporary French writer combines such a breadth and depth of talent, although some may have excelled him in certain spheres. He is a much more stimulating theorician than either Nathalie Sarraute or Robbe-Grillet; thanks to his catholic taste and critical acumen, the three volumes of *Répertoire* are being increasingly quoted by specialists; as a poet, he has immense imaginative gifts; as a writer of prose fiction, he has written two of the best novels in France since 1945, *L'Emploi du temps* and *La Modification*. *Mobile* is that rarity, a wholly successful prototype needing no excuses on the grounds of innovation. A highly significant work, on account of the "mobility" principle, it provides a remarkable reading experience, by turns amusing, depressing, and invigorating. Finally, *Votre Faust* is one of the most interesting experiments since Diaghilev involving a synthesis of the arts.

Butor's importance as a writer, however, transcends the value of any individual text. There can be few of our preconceptions he does not undermine, particularly those leading us to treat facets of experience and expression as isolated compartments: the critical function as separate from the creative, the poetic from the novelistic, the musical from the dramatic. In this destruction of barriers between reader and author, creation and criticism, one art form and another, language is the unifying force and collaboration the tool. In both these respects, Butor's Utopianism may appear no less unreasonable than Utopianism has always been. Although he admires Charles Fourier, he differs from him totally in the imprecision of his forecasts. The future in Fourier's writings is worked out with grotesque exactitude; Butor's fundamental optimism leaves the details to others. No answer is ever supplied to the question which must inevitably be posed after his assertion that life must be changed: in what direction? On the other hand, as Butor maintains in the *Entretiens*, "one must first diagnose the ailment" (p. 81). In the face of the disharmony between language and society, which he sees as the primary ailment, it is perhaps not so unreasonable to be a Utopian, to have faith in something, instead of acquiescing to chaos. In a more positive sense, by his promotion of the "open" work of art, Butor refuses the impasse into which so much contemporary French writing appears to lead.

Notes and References

Chapter One

1. R.-M. Albérès, *Michel Butor* (Editions Universitaires, Coll. "Classiques du XXe siècle," 1964). This and all subsequent works in French are published in Paris unless otherwise stated.

2. Quoted in *Le Monde*, May 23, 1968. See also the numbers of May 24, June 29, 1968, and June 21, 1969 (a retrospective account).

3. Printed in *Textes* ("Union des Ecrivains"), 1969.

4. See Butor in Madeleine Chapsal, *Les Ecrivains en personne* (Julliard, 1960), p. 67.

5. Georges Raillard, *Butor* (Gallimard, Coll. "La Bibliothèque idéale," 1968), p. 39 *passim*.

6. *Répertoire II* (Editions de Minuit, 1964), p. 17. Abbreviated hereafter to *R II*.

7. *R II*, pp. 175 and 185.

8. *Répertoire* (Editions de Minuit, 1960), p. 204. Abbreviated hereafter to *R*.

9. *R*, p. 27.

10. *R II*, p. 54.

11. *R II*, pp. 137–38.

12. E.g., "this profound unease . . . this night in which we struggle" (*R*, p. 9); "an almost furious world assailing us from all sides" (*R*, p. 272).

13. *R*, p. 7; *R II*, p. 88; *ibid.*, p. 294.

14. *Répertoire III* (Editions de Minuit, 1968), p. 8. Abbreviated hereafter to *R III*.

15. *R III*, p. 392.

16. *R II*, p. 88. See also *R III*, p. 8: "The library gives us a world, but it gives us a false world. . . ."

17. Butor in Georges Charbonnier, *Entretiens avec Michel Butor* (Gallimard, 1967), p. 25 (it may be assumed that in any quotation Butor is speaking); See also *R II*, p. 15.

18. Butor is thus critical of the use of a "traditional" style in a contemporary context, or the notion of literature as a means of passing time (*R II*, p. 90; *ibid.*, p. 298).

19. *R*, p. 236.

20. *R III*, p. 242. See also Butor's study of Rousseau, which takes the refractive nature of Lake Geneva as one of its principal metaphors (*R III*, pp. 59–101).

21. *R III*, p. 309.

22. *R*, p. 270.

23. For alliteration, see *R*, p. 223: "Now alliteration . . . is the poetic procedure *par excellence* since its essence is to make language tend toward that ideal of absolute coherence in which meaning and sound are at last solidly linked by laws."

24. *R II*, p. 14.

25. *R II*, p. 18.

26. *Ibid.*

27. *R II*, p. 19.

28. *R*, p. 272.

29. *R*, p. 8: "Whereas the true story has always the support, the resource of external evidence, the novel must be capable of creating what it is telling us about. That is why it is the phenomenological domain *par excellence,* the place *par excellence* in which we can study the way in which reality appears to us or can appear to us: that is why the novel is the laboratory of the narrative." See also *R II*, p. 89.

30. *R*, pp. 79–93.

31. *R*, pp. 271–72.

32. *R II*, p. 90.

33. Maurice Merleau-Ponty, *La Phénoménologie de la perception* (Gallimard, Coll. "Bibliothèque des Idées," 1945), Avant-propos, p.v.

34. See Merleau-Ponty, *op. cit.,* pp. 369–70: "the object is the correlative of my body and in more general sense of my existence, of which my body is only the stabilized structure . . . if we wish to describe reality as it appears to us in our perceptive experience, we find it laden with anthropological attributes. As relationships between objects or various aspects of objects are always mediated by our body, the whole of nature is a staging of our own life, or our own interlocutor in a kind of dialogue. This is why, in the last analysis, we cannot conceive an object that is not perceived or perceptible."

35. *R II*, p. 49.

36. *R II*, p. 17: "A civilization in which sacred elements play their role perfectly, assuring the perfect stability of the profane, is what anthropologists call a 'primitive society.' . . ."

37. For another, see Chapter 6, p. 97.

38. *R II*, p. 299. See also, *R*, p. 230: "any dream is an interpretation of reality."

39. *R*, p. 206: "In the account of a Dublin day, it is possible to find the whole *Odyssey*. In the midst of contemporary strangeness the ancient myths

take on new form and the relationships they express remain universal and eternal" (essay on James Joyce).

40. *R III*, pp. 17–18.

41. Quoted in F. Van Rossum-Guyon, *Critique du roman* (Gallimard, Coll. "Bibliothèque des Idées," 1970), p. 10.

42. *La Modification,* ed. John Sturrock (London, Methuen, 1971), p. vii.

43. Eco's work first appeared in Italian in 1962 and was translated into French in 1965 as *L'Œuvre ouverte* (Editions du Seuil).

44. *R II*, p. 107.

45. *R III*, p. 401 : "The modern book, formed of superimposed leaves, is so designed as to permit a much greater freedom of research within the text [than that afforded by microfilm]; the microfilm can only replace it when a means of 'turning it over' as easily has been discovered."

46. For a useful definition of reader participation in Butor, see Jean Roudaut, *Michel Butor ou le livre futur* (Gallimard, Coll. "Le Chemin," 1965), p. 67. An excellent general discussion of the problem can be found in Eco, *L'Œuvre ouverte,* especially pp. 41–66.

47. Jean Roudaut, "Mallarmé et Butor," *Cahiers du Sud,* LVIII, 378–79 (July–October, 1964), 29–33.

48. For one reason behind this admiration, see Chapter 3, p. 62 and note 31.

49. *R II*, p. 240 ("Victor Hugo romancier").

50. "Any finished, shut, full book is . . . a mask, a façade . . ." (*R II*, p. 212: "Babel en creux"); "Any Gospel taken for the Gospel is an Apocrypha" (above, note 49).

51. *R II*, p. 212.

52. *R III*, p. 16: "But it is in no way essential that a writer should have recognized his work as unfinished for the critical imagination to complete it—as it must."

53. Butor compares Mallarmé's "plural" or ambiguous syntax with Boulez' "idea of a work with several possible aspects, consequently inviting direct intervention and participation by the performer . . ." (*R II*, p. 249).

54. Henri Pousseur, "The Question of Order in New Music," *Perspectives of New Music* (Fall-Winter, 1966), 107–8 [trans. David Behrman].

55. *R III*, p. 9.

56. *Entretiens,* pp. 69–71.

57. *R III*, p. 20 ("La Critique et l'invention"). The whole of this essay is well worth reading in connection with most of the points made in the course of the last few pages.

58. Butor notes that "Rousseau, that great patron of literature as expression of the individual, personally understood admirably well to what extent literature is linked to the form of a society" (*R III*, p. 60).

59. *Entretiens.* p. 243: "In what is new and brought to us by the poet, or the critic if he is a poet, there is an opening onto the future which is indomitable, but what it brings us is continuous with something old. In anything new, there is an aspect open onto the future, and light shed on the past. . . ."

60. *R,* pp. 193–94 ("La Crise de croissance de la science-fiction").

61. *L'Arc,* 39 (1969). Quotations from pp. 1–4.

62. John Sturrock, *The French New Novel* (Oxford: O.U.P., 1969), p. 139.

63. For a detailed discussion of Butor's debt to literary Surrealism, see Chapter 8, pp. 151–54.

Chapter Two

1. Published by Gallimard, 1967, subtitled "capriccio."

2. *Portrait,* p. 60: "rather than claim to remember the dreams I could have had at the château de H. well enough to be able to note them down after so many years, I prefer to construct them deliberately, dreaming methodically of those vanished dreams of yesteryear." As regards the "waking" Butor, see Jacqueline Piatier, "Butor s'explique," *Le Monde,* March 22, 1967, where the author agrees that the book is autobiographical, but "a constructed autobiography. . . . Any autobiography is a construction."

3. J. Piatier, *op. cit.*

4. *See Arabian Nights,* "The History of the second Calendar, the Son of a King."

5. And/or a "vendeuse" (saleswoman, p. 83). It is not clear whether both live there, he has visited her, or vice versa.

6. Analyzed in most detail by Jennifer Walters, "Symbolism in *Passage de Milan,*" *French Review,* XLII, 2 (December, 1968), 223–32.

7. For "fog," "smoke," etc., see especially *L'Emploi du temps* (Chapter 3, note 28).

8. pp. 13, 35, 56, 73, 76, 99, 135.

9. pp. 9–11, 21–22, 72–73, etc.

10. In view of the obvious decrepitude of the educational system to which he belongs (see pp. 16–17: a prefiguration of *Degrés*), this is perhaps not surprising.

11. See pp. 150, 164, 284. See also Chapter 4, pp. 78–79, and note 28.

12. And, of course, the "passage" from life to death for Angèle, and from a routine existence to a new one in the case of Louis Lécuyer. For the theme of "passage" in *La Modification,* see F. Van Rossum-Guyon, *Critique du roman,* pp. 269–77.

13. J. Walters, *art. cit.,* 230, and her note 8.

14. Another play on words? (vere/verre [glass]=clarity as opposed to opacity [see Chapter 3, p. 60 and note 28]).

15. Henri Pousseur in *Les Cahiers du centre d'études et de recherches marxistes,* 62 (1962), p. 52.

16. See Chapter 1, pp. 28–29, and note 51.

17. See Chapter 1, p. 19, and note 19.

18. "Sand" and "cinders" are often used by Butor to indicate in a broad sense failure and, more precisely, physical infirmity. "At that time my vision was still like unclouded water; since then, every day has cast in its pinch of ashes," writes Jacques Revel at the beginning of *L'Emploi du temps* (p. 10); the hero of *Portrait de l'artiste* dreams that he is rendered sightless in one eye by a cinder (p. 198); Léon Delmont realizes that "our love is not a road leading somewhere, but [that] it is destined to become lost in the sands of our mutual aging" (*La Modification,* p. 272).

19. Bachelard, *L'Eau et les rêves* (Corti, 1942), p. 125.

20. pp. 48, 55, 71, 74, 75, 81, 91, 96, 103, 105, 124, 179, 182, 256, 273.

21. In phenomenological terms, this is an indication of the author's struggle to achieve an "optimum distance" (Merleau-Ponty, *La Phéno-ménologie de la perception,* p. 348 *et seq.*)

22. The poet Francis Ponge uses a similar technique for similar purposes in, e.g., *Le Parti pris des choses.*

Chapter Three

1. Page references in this chapter will refer to the "10/18" edition, which includes an excellent analysis of the novel by Georges Raillard, part of which has since been incorporated in his general study of Butor's work. The frequent misprints in this edition have been corrected where necessary.

2. One of Revel's many problems, indicating his exclusion, in his difficulty in finding open restaurants or palatable food. See pp. 12, 18, 26, 45, 115, 266, 356.

3. *Butor,* p. 26.

4. Jenkins' mother, with whom he lives, is the daughter of the subject for the statues sculpted in the porches of the New Cathedral.

5. By the use of "perhaps," or "rather," a second or third noun or verb, often in parentheses, etc.

6. G. Raillard, see "10/18" edition pp. 463–70; *Butor,* esp. pp. 100–107. Spitzer in *Archivum Linguisticum,* XIII, 12 (1961), 171–95.

7. There are two exceptions to this: Saturday, June 7 (Revel continues his account of the visit to the Old Cathedral the previous November), and Sunday, August 30 or 31 (see below, note 8)—Rose and Lucien have just become engaged.

8. On "Sunday, August 30," Revel relates how he learned the news the previous day. But September 1 is a Monday (?) Has the shock caused him to forget the date?

9. On the formal level, the events of March would in any case be related in October, after Revel has left Bleston.

10. The sky at Bleston is frequently described in terms of metal. See pp. 73, 74, 79, 233, etc.

11. In Sartre's *La Nausée*, some of Roquentin's conclusions about experience are shared by his former mistress, Anny, although she has reached them by a less nightmarish route.

12. Presumably all the tickets are *burned* after their collection. Each one bears a strict injunction to "REMEMBER [*sic*] . . . that this garden is a place for relaxation, not disorderly behavior: behave in a proper manner on all occasions" (p. 207), a very Draconian message, even for a Lancashire park! The word "REMEMBER" may well have begun a process culminating only a fortnight later in the decision to keep a diary, while Revel's act in burning the ticket appears to be a ritual protestation against the rules of the city in which he is trapped.

13. See Chapter 1, p. 18.

14. ". . . that far too great a distance which I was hoping rapidly to reduce . . . daily becomes in a way thicker, more opaque" (p. 187). See also p. 319: "water seven months deep, less and less transparent because agitation has stirred up the slime."

15. ". . . all those early winter days which I had already tried to anchor with this long, reticular chain of sentences . . ." (p. 374).

16. Leo Spitzer, *art. cit.*, 195.

17. W. M. Frohock, *André Malraux and the Tragic Imagination* (California: Stanford U.P., 1952; reprinted in paperback form, 1967), esp. pp. 65 and 110.

18. *Butor*, p. 83 *et seq.*

19. *R*, p. 214 (study of James Joyce, who was strongly influenced by Vico).

20. Jean Roudaut has some very pertinent remarks on Cain and fire symbolism in his *Michel Butor ou le livre futur*, pp. 156–72.

21. References to buildings damaged or destroyed by fire: pp. 167–68, 178, 188, 201, 209, 242, etc. See also note 28.

22. *R*. pp. 262–70 ("Une Autobiographie dialectique"). Quotations pp. 265–66.

23. *R III*, pp. 351–69 ("Les Mosquées de New York ou l'art de Mark Rothko").

24. *Cahiers du Sud*, 1956. Reprinted in *R*, pp. 7–11 ("Le Roman comme recherche"). Quotation p. 11.

25. See Chapter 1, p. 23.

26. L. Spitzer, *art. cit.* Spitzer's analysis of the novel's style (pp. 191–95) has proved invaluable to the present writer.

27. The very first sentence ("The gleams spread everywhere") takes on

fuller significance when Revel's task of replacing obscurity by light is understood.

28. Ocular (the imagery of eyes/sight/blindness), e.g., pp. 10, 36, 42, 45, 47, 55, 72, 166, 176, 242, 271, 277, 305–6, 350, 370, 375, 389, 396; igneous (burned buildings, Cain and fire, Revel's passion), eg., pp. 9, 10, 21, 39, 47, 57, 77, 108 *passim* (Cain), 123, 134, 167–68, 170, 178–79, 188, 201, 204, 209, 227, 231, 242, 254, 265, 271, 277, 296, 311, 324, 329–30, 332 *passim*, 353–54, 356, 363, 370, 378, 387, 394–95, 405, 417, 435; liquid (water, beer, rum, *not* including the references, in practically every entry of Revel's diary, to Bleston's incessant rain), e.g., pp. 10, 17, 32, 35, 39, 40, 53, 61, 70, 117, 166, 170, 176, 178, 212, 294, 319, 374; atmospheric (Bleston's poisoned air and smoke, the pure sky of Crete, etc.), e.g., pp. 11, 41, 45, 48, 77, 145–46, 166, 170, 247, 272, 277, 289, 303, 305, 314, 324, 328, 332, 346, 359, 396, 407, 412.

29. F. Van Rossum-Guyon, *Critique du roman*, chapter V.

30. *R II*, p. 22.

31. Significantly, "Babel en creux" (*R II*, pp. 199–214) defends what is normally regarded as one of the worst features of Hugo's poetry: "Thus this juxtaposition of proper names is in no sense a vain display of useless erudition, but a means of forming monster-words, of setting up, between words we understand and those we misunderstand, a link that will enable them to swarm, crawl, spread out, a continuous immersion of the famous ones in the mass of forgotten ones from which they stand out" (p. 204). See also, apropos of note 30 above: "Pointless to try and single out the fine line here ... one must obviously grasp this system in its flow, in its avalanche, in the totality of its movements" (p. 210).

32. *La Préciosité et les précieux* (Nizet, 1960), p. 314.

33. For Butor and alchemy, see J. H. Matthews in *Un nouveau roman?* (*Revue des lettres modernes*, 1964 (1), nos. 94–99, pp. 51–66).

Chapter Four

1. *La Modification* (Editions de Minuit, 1957). References throughout this chapter will again be to the "10/18" edition, with the same warning about misprints (corrected where necessary) and the same commendation of the postface, this time by Michel Leiris.

2. For other treatments of this theme and general parallels with other novels see J. K. Simon, "View from the Train: Butor, Gide, Larbaud," *French Review*, XXXVI, 2 (December, 1962), 161–66, and F. Van Rossum-Guyon, *Critique du roman*, pp. 177–86.

3. *Répertoire* was awarded the "prix de la critique littéraire" in 1960.

4. Delmont's reading of the letters of Julian the Apostate (pp. 102, 205, 207, 218, 253, 275) can either be interpreted as a token of his hatred

for Roman Catholicism or his ambiguous attitude toward it. In spite of Julian's apostasy, it has been held that, on his deathbed, he discussed the immortality of the soul and cried: "Thou hast conquered, O Galilean."

5. *Butor,* p. 265.

6. L. S. Roudiez argues in his *Michel Butor* (New York: Columbia Essays on Modern Writers, 9, 1965), p. 19, that *La Modification* is basically an existentialist novel about the replacement of bad faith (Delmont's failure to respond to the challenge of his situation with Henriette) by an authentic choice to stay with his wife. But in view of his cowardice and procrastination, it is difficult to accept the notion of an authentic choice. His talk of determinism is what constitutes his bad faith.

7. See R.-M. Albérès, *Butor,* p. 72, for this analogy.

8. *R II,* p. 96 ("Recherches sur la technique du roman").

9. Several fellow passengers also possess books: the priest has a breviary, the young couple a *Blue Guide* and an Italian *Assimil,* the professor his law books, etc.

10. The photographs in the compartment are another object affecting Delmont's mind, suggesting a freer, romantic life. See Leo Spitzer, "Quelques aspects de la technique des romans de Michel Butor," *Archivum linguisticum,* XIV, 1 (1962), 49–76.

11. He has also read Book I in Rome a year earlier (pp. 261–62).

12. R.-M. Albérès, p. 72: "Léon Delmont doesn't reason...."

13. M. Merleau-Ponty, *La Phénoménologie de la perception,* p. 491, quoted in I. W. Alexander, "The Phenomenological Philosophy in France," *Currents of Thought in French Literature* (Oxford: Blackwell, 1965), pp. 325–51.

14. *La Phénoménologie de la perception,* p. 496.

15. *Op. cit.,* p. 517: "Thus neither determinism nor absolute choice ever exist...."

16. I am indebted to a research student, Mrs. A. Tamuly, for this observation. Delmont's talk of "determinism" is thus no more than an example of bad faith.

17. See Chapter 1, p. 23.

18. See *Le Génie du lieu* (Grasset, 1958), pp. 48–51 on Athens and Salonika. I am therefore unable to accept Georges Raillard's reference to the "heterogeneity, which cannot be simplified, of the various stages in the 'continuity of Rome'" (*Butor,* p. 131). Michel Leiris' assertion that "Rome has a permanence transcending its changes" (*La Modification,* p. 296) seems far more tenable.

19. See also *Le Génie du lieu,* pp. 97–98 for similar remarks in connection with the city of Mantua.

20. "We must not hope for any fixed state, unless it be a false one. At every moment we must redefine our position in space and time, reinvent

ourselves, so to speak." (Jean Roudaut, "Répétition et modification dans deux romans de Michel Butor," *Saggi e ricerche di letterature francese,* VIII (1967), 364.

21. *R II,* pp. 42–50 ("L'Espace du roman"), esp. p. 49; and pp. 51–60 ("Philosophie de l'ameublement").

22. L. Spitzer, *art. cit.,* p. 50.

23. The following analysis of the novel's structure owes a good deal to Jean Roudaut's essay (above, note 20).

24. F. Van Rossum-Guyon works on a rather different system, in that she discerns five and not seven "time-strophes" (*Critique du roman,* pp. 215–77).

25. E.g. pp. 71–84 (b) contain layers (k) (pp. 74 and 82), (a) (pp. 74, 75), and (d) (p. 74).

26. Pp. 116, 137, 152, 182, 204, 211, 219 (Charon posing the same questions), 232, 252 (a series of questions, most of which have already been put by the "Great Huntsman").

27. Pp. 206–7, 211, 214–215, 218–20, 231–33. I have no idea why *all* the dream passages are not related as happening to a kind of depersonalized Delmont.

28. See also, e.g., pp. 47 ("cracking"), 58 ("splits"), 134 ("tears"), 182 ("abyss"), 281 ("fault"), etc.

29. *Figaro littéraire,* December 7, 1957. Quoted by Michel Leiris in his postface to *La Modification,* p. 311.

30. First published in *Les Temps modernes,* XVI, 178 (February, 1961), 936–48. Reprinted in *R II,* pp. 61–72.

31. "Narrative 'you' in Contemporary Literature," *Comparative Literature Studies,* II, 1 (1965), 1–24.

32. "The voice which says *vous* is less that of the character than of the author, or, better still, that of a *persona,* invisible but powerfully present, who serves as the center of consciousness in the novel" (Morrissette, p. 15).

33. M. Albérès manages this best (?): "since the entire novel is written in the second person ... we therefore become Léon Delmont ..." (*Butor,* p. 68).

34. This possibility is well presented by L. S. Roudiez, *Michel Butor,* p. 21.

Chapter Five

1. Sartre in Madeleine Chapal, *Les Ecrivains en personne* (Julliard, 1960), p. 217.

2. L. S. Roudiez, *Michel Butor,* p. 23.

3. "I wonder if in all great novels there isn't that idea of sacrifice ..." (Butor in F. C. St. Aubyn, "Entretien avec Michel Butor," *French Review,* XXXVI, 1 (October, 1962), 12–22).

4. See F. Rabelais, *Œuvres complètes*, ed. Pierre Jourda (Garnier. 1962). Tome 1, Introduction, pp. XXIX–XXX.

5. This is in no way meant as a criticism of these magazines, especially *Galaxie*, which is concerned with science-fiction. On the contrary, Butor would presumably far sooner have these on the syllabus than some of the more traditional offerings.

6. E.g. p. 270: the *Odyssey, Livy, Britannicus, Fiction;* p. 275: *Fiction, Galaxie, Iliad, Odyssey, Lettres Persanes.*

7. Daval, pp. 37 and 38; Mouron, p. 39; Régnier, pp. 111–12; Hutter, pp. 68–70, 76–77, 92, 152–53.

8. Butor also frequently quotes, for ironical effect, the passage from Gargantua's letter to Pantagruel: "all the plants of the earth, all the various metals that are hid within the cavernous bowels, the precious stones of all the East and South, let nothing be unknown to thee" (replacing Rabelais' "te" ["thee"] by "lui" ["him"]).

9. Wolves feature prominently in Butor's poetry with a similar rôle. Just before his outburst precipitating Vernier's final defeat, his nephew Pierre Eller imagines he is turning into one (p. 382).

10. M. de Montaigne, *Essais,* ed. Tilley and Boase (Manchester: Manchester U.P., 1954), p. 176.

11. But see Raymond Jean's remarks on the absence of bustle and "ragging" in *La Littérature et le réel* (Albin Michel, 1965), p. 223.

12. Jean Roudaut, "Répétition et modification dans deux romans de Michel Butor," *Saggi e ricerche di letteratura francese,* VIII (1967), 311–64.

13. The title of *Degrés* is of course richly ambiguous: degrees of parentage (p. 141), of exactitude in knowledge (p. 119), on any kind of scale (*Vernier,* etc.); in general, it suggests regular progression, as befits the novel's structure.

14. John Sturrock, *The French New Novel,* p. 136.

15. J. Roudaut, *art. cit.,* pp. 345–46: "What matters to him [Vernier] is less the collecting of facts than the establishment of precisely how they are linked."

16. J. Roudaut, pp. 335–37.

17. See also *Degrés,* pp. 149–50, 186.

18. Butor in St. Aubyn, *art. cit.,* p. 13.

19. Jean Ricardou, "Michel Butor ou le roman et ses degrés," *NRF,* XV, 90 (June, 1960), 1157–61.

20. The whole forms a splendid example of bad faith allied to the phenomenological process of "imaginary variation."

21. See especially pp. 198–99, 216–18, 256–62, 270–71, 278–83.

22. J. Sturrock, *op. cit.,* p. 130.

23. F. C. St. Aubyn, "Michel Butor and Phenomenological Realism,"

Studi Francesi, XVI (January–April, 1962), 51–62. Quotation p. 62.

24. Sturrock, p. 139.

Chapter Six

1. This was already written when Leon S. Roudiez kindly sent me his excellent "Problems of Point of View in the Early Fiction of Michel Butor," *Kentucky Romance Quarterly,* XVIII, 2 (1971), 145–59, in which the variations of point of view in the four novels are discussed in the context of Eco's theory of the "open" work.

2. G. Charbonnier, *Entretiens avec Michel Butor,* p. 195. The best analysis of Butor's conception of the individual is by Rodolphe Roelens, "Une recherche psychologique méconnue: le courant 'dramatique' de Georges Politzer à aujourd'hui," *La Pensée,* no. 103 (May–June, 1962), 76–101.

3. See Chapter 1, p. 27.

4. Roland Barthes, "Littérature et discontinu," *Critique,* XVIII, 185 (October, 1962), 817–29, reprinted in *Essais ctitiques* (Seuil, 1964), pp. 175–87.

5. See Chapter 1, p. 30.

6. See Chapter 1, p. 28 and note 49.

7. The main motive for quotation in *Mobile* is gross disrespect, however. See the references to Jefferson and Carnegie in this chapter.

8. *R II,* p. 294.

9. All these points are found in "Le livre comme objet" (*R II,* pp. 104–23). See also "Sur la page" (*ibid.,* pp. 100–103); "Monument de rien pour Apollinaire" (*R III,* pp. 269–305); "La littérature, l'oreille et l'œil" (*ibid.,* pp. 391–403).

10. The ambiguity of the work's title is obvious: Mobile is a well-known city in Alabama, the first state treated in *Mobile;* movement or travel from state to state by automobile is one of the principal American activities revealed by Butor's book; above all, *Mobile* alludes to the mobility of the text.

11. For influences on *Mobile* see W. M. Frohock, "Faulkner and the 'roman nouveau' [*sic*]: an Interim Report," *Bucknell Review,* X, 3 (1962), 186–93; Catharine Savage Brosman, "A Source and Parallel of Michel Butor's 'Mobile': 'In the American Grain,'" *Modern Language Review,* LXVI, 2 (April, 1971), 315–21; and "Michel Butor and *Paterson*," *Forum for Modern Language Studies,* VII, 2 (April, 1971), 126–33. There are also several parallels to be drawn between the novels of Dos Passos and Butor's work.

12. Butor has outlined *Mobile*'s construction at considerable length to F. C. St. Aubyn, in the latter's "A propos de *Mobile:* deuxième entretien avec Michel Butor," *French Review,* XXXVIII, 4 (February, 1965), 427–40. See also *Entretiens,* pp. 156–64.

13. R. Barthes, *Essais critiques*, p. 180.

14. There are many exceptions to this, particularly in the case of the more lyrical components of the text, which may spread over the entire page.

15. "Now as every city in the United States was founded on a recent murder, forgotten with difficulty but vigorously, the assassination of Lincoln was a strikingly successful representation of this foundation murder" (*Mobile*, pp. 135–36).

16. See Chapter 1, p. 17.

17. V. Laternani, *Movimenti religiosi dei popoli oppressi*, quoted in *Mobile*, pp. 92–96, 106–7, 167, 182, 220–26, etc.

18. Pp. 41–43, 120–24, 274–77, 308–15.

19. Thomas Jefferson, *Notes on the State of Virginia*, ed. William Peden (Univ. North Carolina Press, 1955), p. 143; *Mobile*, p. 43 is a translation of p. 138; pp. 120–24=pp. 138–40; pp. 274–77=pp. 140–41; pp. 308–15= pp. 141–43. I have replaced Butor's translation by the original English.

20. Letter dated August 30, 1791, quoted by Peden, p. 287; Dos Passos, *The Head and Heart of Thomas Jefferson* (New York: Doubleday, 1954), p. 388.

21. *Entretiens*, pp. 219–21. Quotations in *Mobile:* Penn, pp. 73–74, 77, 79, 133; Franklin, pp. 74, 77, 79, 133, 187–89, 209–11, 243–44, 247–48, 250–51, 317, 322; Carnegie, pp. 243–44, 246–47, 250.

22. Andrew Carnegie, *The Gospel of Wealth*, ed. E. C. Kirkland (Belknap Press of Harvard U.P., 1962), pp. 71–73.

23. For a long discussion on the rôle of colors in the American consciousness, see *Entretiens*, pp. 168–84.

24. Lucien Goldmann, "Nouveau roman et réalité," in *Pour une Sociologie du roman* (Gallimard, Coll. "Bibliothèque des idées", 1964), p. 193.

25. *R III*, p. 355 ("Les Mosquées de New York ou l'art de Mark Rothko").

26. Pp. 71–72. See also pp. 174–75, juxtaposition of nylon knicker colors and "painting by numbers" scenes.

27. *Entretiens*, p. 171: "Each of these lists is a kind of matrix, and we can multiply one by another and produce a total number of images engendered by these two factors. Their confrontation allows us to open the doors to new recesses of our imagination."

28. *Mobile*, p. 263 (quotation from H. P. Lovecraft).

29. R.-M. Albérès, *Butor*, p. 93.

30. Roland Barthes, *Essais critiques*, p. 176.

31. Another interesting phenomenon is withdrawal, a desperate clinging to "the old way of life" by pretending that one is not really living in a foreign country at all. This is indicated in *Mobile* by the

frequency of European place names, with or without the prefix "new."

32. *R II*, p. 165 ("Chateaubriand et l'ancienne Amérique").

33. "The problem of the United States is the problem of what happens to European civilization when it settles in a land that allows it to develop on a larger scale" (*Entretiens*, p. 231).

Chapter Seven

1. See Jean Roudaut's analysis of *6 810 000 Litres* ("Parenthèse sur la place occupée par l'étude intitulée '6 810 000 litres d'eau par seconde' parmi les autres ouvrages de Michel Butor," *NRF*, XXVIII, 165 (December, 1966), 498–509).

2. See below, pp. 131–32.

3. Through the "Union des écrivains." See Chapter 1, p. 16, and *Le Monde*, June 29, 1968: "Les Buts de l' 'Union des écrivains'."

4. In *Illustrations II* (Gallimard, 1969), Butor quotes *himself* extensively by intermingling a number of his own poems already published separately elsewhere.

5. See *R III*, pp. 383–90 ("L'Opéra c'est-à-dire le théâtre").

6. *R III*, pp. 391–403, especially pp. 391–92.

7. *Les Mots dans la peinture* (Geneva: Skira, Coll. "Les Sentiers de la création," 1969). Quotation p. 174.

8. For Montaigne, see *Essais sur les Essais* (Gallimard, Coll. "Les Essais," 1968), p. 208; Rousseau, see *R III*, pp. 59–101, esp. pp. 77–80; Monet, *ibid.*, pp. 241–58, and my Chapter 1, pp. 19–20.

9. See below, p. 156.

10. To be more accurate, those who do replace it are not given dialogues. The plane is not necessarily empty just because only one or two "speaking" couples remain.

11. There are exceptions to this. Couple E–g suddenly appears on plane five (Teheran-Orly), between Athens and Orly, although no stop at Athens has been indicated. This is presumably to avoid too much duplication of stops which have already been made by planes on their outward journey.

12. The only typographical point of interest is the use of italics to indicate that the planes concerned are enveloped in night.

13. It is tempting to seek an over-all, mathematical pattern governing the plane sequences. I am grateful to a former colleague, Dr. J. H. Conway, Lecturer in Mathematics at Cambridge University, for examining various examples of "almost periodicity" in plane sequences, and for assuring me that there is no over-all pattern, only local ones.

14. See L. S. Roudiez, *Michel Butor*, p. 37: "The total impression is one of a choral song of mankind in which unidentified individuals blend

their common preoccupations about different things and countries into elemental melodies of love and hate."

15. See also pp. 86–87 (A–j), 89 (*ibid.*), 92 (*ibid.*), etc.

16. Minerals: pp. 27, 35, 41, 47, 74, 81, 84, 93–94, 97, 104, 108, 119. Phoenix: pp. 67, 68, 71, 77, 80, 87, 107.

17. See *R*, pp. 12–19 ("L'Alchimie et son langage"), and *Portrait de l'artiste en jeune singe, passim.*

18. E in particular (plane ten) has hated every minute of his stay (p. 60).

19. A (plane one) lists the stages out (pp. 108–9), while his companion, j, can only think of the stages back (p. 112).

20. *Description de San Marco* (Gallimard, 1963).

21. John Sturrock, *The French New Novel*, pp. 109–110, has some very pertinent remarks on water and memory in *San Marco.*

22. John Ruskin, *Works*, ed. Cook and Wedderburn (London: Allen, 1904), Vol. X, *The Stones of Venice* (Vol. II), Chapter 4, pp. 69–142; Vol. XXIV, *St. Mark's Rest*, Chapter 9 (edited by J. Ruskin), pp. 309–34. Abbreviated hereafter to *SV* and *SMR.*

23. See also p. 112: "the whole edifice is to be regarded less as a temple wherein to pray, than as itself a Book of Common Prayer, a vast illuminated missal, bound with alabaster instead of parchment, studded with porphyry pillars instead of jewels, and written within and without in letters of enamel and gold."

24. Butor, *San Marco*, pp. 92–101; Ruskin, *SMR*, pp. 282–85 and 309–34. Ruskin's version, it must be stressed, is written up from notes, and was not originally intended for publication.

25. E.g., the Adoration scene (from the Infancy of Christ) is described in detail by Ruskin (*SMR*, p. 320), while Butor concentrates on the relatively insignificant detail of a servant leading a camel, and on the star (*San Marco*, p. 92); Butor omits scenes of St. John's life (in the desert, receiving a cloak from the angel, preaching); he fails to respect the hierarchical order of the three heavenly agencies (compare *SMR*, pp. 332–33 with *San Marco*, pp. 98–99); the cycles of mosaics are inextricably mixed; and so on.

26. For Butor's comments on this, see *Entretiens*, pp. 177–78.

27. See also pp. 29, 32, 51, 53–54, 60, 93–94, 97, 99–100, 111–12.

28. *6 810 000 Litres d'eau par seconde, étude stéréophonique* (Gallimard, 1965). A version for the theater was presented on the stage of Wogensky's "théâtre tournant" at the Grenoble "Maison de Culture" shortly after its opening in 1968. See *Le Monde*, February 15, 1968, for a brief account by Jean Lacouture.

29. Sections as follows: "Introduction"; "The Couples"; "The Blacks"; "The Bridal Veil" (part of the American Falls); "The Illuminations"; "The Hotel Rooms"; "The Awakenings"; "The Fogs"; "The Phantoms";

"The Styx"; "The Cold"; "Coda." The itineraries ("voies") are numbered "A" to "J." With "A," one follows only the basic text, without any parentheses, with "B" one reads a little more, and so on until the entire work is covered by following "J."

30. Couples as follows: "old couple"; "just married" [in English in text]; "black gardeners"; "mutton dressed as lamb" and "gigolo"; "dastardly seducer" and "easy victim"; "white married woman" and "white married man"; "lonely young man" (alone, or in apposition to "lonely young woman"); "widower" (alone, or with "widow").

31. This is confirmed by Butor in the *Entretiens,* pp. 144–45.

32. Many fragments of dialogue are also recapitulated, e.g., "There wasn't that enormous tower like a water-tower" (pp. 26/274); "Your hands covered in earth . . ." (pp. 57/277).

33. For a detailed analysis of this development, see my article in *Australian Journal of French Studies,* VI, 1 (1969), 101–12.

34. In the original, Andrew's voice is to the right, and that of the reader in the middle.

35. E.g., pp. 53–57, 113–15, 155–57. Elsewhere, it is frequently uncertain whether colors refer to flowers or the illuminated Falls, an example of deliberate ambiguity, according to Butor (*Entretiens,* p. 183).

36. Georges Raillard, *Butor,* p. 181.

37. The previous year, Pousseur's article, "Vers un nouvel univers sonore", was published in the same number of *Esprit* (no. 280, January, 1960) as Butor's "La Musique: art réaliste"; this coincidence may well have marked the beginning of their awareness that they had much in common.

38. For a more complete list of extracts, see my article in *Australian Journal of French Studies,* VIII, 1 (1971), 84–97. Since this was written, I have discovered two more.

39. *R II,* pp. 27–41 ("La Musique: art réaliste").

40. Interview in June, 1967, with J.-Y. Bosseur, reproduced in *Votre Faust,* in *Les Cahiers du centre d'études et de recherches marxistes,* no. 62 (1968), esp. pp. 32–35.

41. *R III,* p. 386 ("L'Opéra c'est-à-dire le théâtre").

42. Henri Pousseur, "The Question of Order in New Music," *Perspectives of New Music* (Fall-Winter, 1966), 93–111.

43. Umberto Eco, *L'Œuvre ouverte,* p. 9.

44. Ernst Bloch, *Das Prinzip Hoffnung,* Vol. 1 (Frankfurt am Main: Suhrkamp Verlag, 1959), section 30 "Die Schaubühne, als paradigmatische Anstalt betrachtet, und die Entscheidung in ihr"—"The theatre seen as a paradigmatic and decision-provoking institution").

45. *R II,* p. 28.

46. *Cahiers,* p. 15.

47. For full details, see *Médiations,* 6 (Summer, 1963), 7–10. For the general staging arrangements, see *ibid.,* 5–6.

48. See *Cahiers,* pp. 53–65, for a detailed account by Pousseur of the procedure of musical quotation and its effect on the "style" of each variant.

49. *NRF,* XIX, 109 (January, 1962), 82; see also p. 71 and *ibid.,* XIX, 110 (February, 1962), 272.

50. This may also be an ironical extension of the frequent Butorian theme of a work of art describing its own creation, since here, of course, the fictional Henri never writes a single note.

Chapter Eight

1. *Où, Le Génie du lieu, 2* (Gallimard, 1971).

2. *La Rose des vents, 32 Rhumbs pour Charles Fourier* (Gallimard, Coll. "Le Chemin," 1970) [literally: *The Mariner's Card, 32 Rhumbs for Charles Fourier*]. A "rhumb" is "the line followed by a vessel sailing on one course or a wind blowing continuously in one direction" or "any one of the set of lines drawn through a point on a map or chart and indicating the course of an object moving always in the same direction."

3. *Dialogue avec 33 variations de Ludwig van Beethoven sur une valse de Diabelli* (Gallimard, Coll. "Le Chemin," 1971).

4. *Travaux d'approche* (Gallimard, Coll. "Poésie," 1972).

5. Thanks to these upheavals, the municipal library at Nice has acquired a large number of books and typescripts forming the nucleus of the "Fonds Michel Butor." See Chronology for 1972.

6. "One never knows with him what is image, humor, or definite affirmation," writes Simone Debout, Fourier, *Œuvres complètes* (Editions Anthropos, 1966), Vol. 1, Intro., p. xxvi.

7. H. Juin, "Présence de Charles Fourier dans la poésie moderne," *Topique,* 4–5 (October, 1970), 124. Butor first heard of Zuñi in 1949, in the company of Breton (*Où,* p. 347).

8. There is a scholarly edition by Jean Gaulmier (Klincksieck, 1961).

9. See R. Barthes, *Sade, Fourier, Loyola* (Seuil, 1971). Most of the material on Fourier first appeared in *Critique,* 281 (October, 1970). Fourier is first mentioned by Butor in *Histoire extraordinaire* (Gallimard, 1961), pp. 99–102.

10. E.g., p. 153.

11. As Butor points out (p. 15) Fourier either includes or adds the pivot of the series, which allows him to count 32 or 33, 134 or 135, etc.

12. S. Debout (above, note 6), p. xx.

13. H. Juin (above, note 7), 103–25, esp. 108–13. The number of *Topique* in which this appears also contains a delightfully baroque homage-poem to

Fourier by Butor entitled "La Politique des charmeuses" (pp. 99–101), based on a story in Fourier's *La fausse Industrie.*

14. See below, p. 157. For Fourier's use of analogies, see *Œuvres complètes,* Vol. IV, pp. 212–41 and VI, pp. 459–67.

15. Fourier is at least kind enough to justify the disposition (*Œuvres complètes,* Vol. II, p. 54 (second pagination) *et seq.*

16. *Charles Fourier, ou la contestation globale* (Seghers, Coll. "Philosophes de tous les temps," 1970), p. 81.

17. S. Debout (above, note 6), p. xxii.

18. H. Pousseur, "The Question of Order in New Music," *Perspectives of New Music* (Fall-Winter, 1966), esp. pp. 107–8 (a discussion of Webern and "overdetermination").

19. See also p. 14.

20. E.g., p. 83: "If the first versant was a meditation on the state of contemporary music, the second will include a meditation on its history. The fantasy of the rays (19) can be considered a deliberate reference to the *Goldberg Variations*," etc.

21. E.g., p. 28: "Besides, if I have named this page the hoar-frost, it is because the theme has been in a way whitened." See also p. 133, etc.

22. E.g., there are 35 views of Mount Sandia ("winter evenings"), divided into 5 groups of 7, each view being composed of 7 "versets."

23. The correct geographical name appears to be the "Sandia Mountains," although Butor always refers to "Mount Sandia." I have respected Butor's appellation.

24. "Sayataca's [=Butor's "Corne-longue"] night chant" and "Night chant of . . . Ca'lako." See Ruth L. Bunzel, "Zuni Ritual Poetry," *Bureau of American Ethnology,* 47th Annual Report, Smithsonian Institution, Washington, D.C., 1932, pp. 611–836 (Sayataca's chant translated pp. 710–21, Shalako's, pp. 762–76).

25. *Où,* p. 177. This is also the title of one of the sacred Mormon books, by Joseph Smith!

26. Marcel Schwob, *Le Livre de Monelle* (Stock, 1923), pp. 111, 116, etc.

27. G. Apollinaire, *La Femme assise* (Editions de la *NRF,* 1920).

28. Presumably Butor did not have space to reproduce the scenes of religious fanaticism described in *La Femme assise,* pp. 121–25.

29. J. Cazeneuve, *Les Dieux dansent à Cibola* (Gallimard, 1957), p. 121, sets out the aims of the ceremony thus: "It is at once a ceremony for the dead, war, and hunting, at the same time as it is mainly designed to bring rain, make the fields fertile, bless the new houses, and give to the entire people happy and long life."

30. Jacqueline Piatier, "Michel Butor entre Beethoven et le Mont Sandia," *Le Monde hebdomadaire,* July 29—August 4, 1971.

31. Bunzel (above, note 24, p. 973) makes the entry of the Shalako into

the village the high point of the ceremonies, while Cazeneuve (above, note 29) does not single out any one aspect.

32. For the passing of time, see, e.g., pp. 12, 30, 52, 63, 149, 221, 245, 283, 312, 344.

33. Hubert Juin, "Tentative de 'lecture' d'un clavier géographique," *Lettres françaises,* June 30, 1971.

34. A detailed analysis of the complicated tense structure of *Où*—which appears to have two "real" presents (at Albuquerque and in the Pyrenees) and several "false" ones—would be well worth attempting.

35. The word "instant" recurs obsessively in *Ŏu,* e.g., p. 329: "all this organizes itself for an instant within the thirst of my gaze."

36. This was written before M. Georges Raillard kindly gave me a copy of his essay on "Référence plastique et discours littéraire chez Michel Butor," *Critique,* 299 (April, 1972), 328–44. Unless I have misread a fascinating but difficult text, his p. 334 is making much the same point.

37. Paul Valéry, *Choses tues II,* in *Œuvres II* (Pléiade, 1960), p. 478.

38. Jean Roudaut. See Chapter 1, p. 28 and note 47.

39. Laurent LeSage, "Michel Butor: Techniques of the Marvelous," *L'Esprit créateur,* VI, 1 (Spring, 1966), 36–44, claims that the surface banality of Butor's novels is a thin cover for an underlying layer of "le merveilleux." P. Aubery, "Surréalisme et littérature actuelle," *Kentucky Romance Quarterly,* XIV, 1 (1967), 33–44, is mainly concerned with the social rôle of literature as envisaged by the Surrealists, Butor, and other modern writers.

40. *R,* pp. 173–85 ("Sur les procédés de Raymond Roussel"); *ibid.,* pp. 262–70 ("Une autobiographie dialectique": Leiris); *R III,* pp. 325–50 ("Héptaedre héliotrope": Breton).

41. "La Peinture surréaliste," *Cahier bicolore* (Laboratoires Roussel, Paris), No. 4 (1963), 23–28.

42. *R,* pp. 12–19 (dated 1953).

43. *R,* p. 146. See Breton, *Second Manifeste du Surréalisme* in *Manifestes du Surréalisme* (Pauvert, 1962), p. 154.

44. See Chapter 7, p. 116 and note 8.

45. See Chapter 1, p. 22 and note 27.

46. See above, note 8.

47. J. Gaulmier, p. 36.

48. *Le Surréalisme et la peinture* (New York: Brentano's, 1945), p. 74. Compare Butor's "Within Surrealism there is Realism . . ." (Chapter 1, p. 25).

49. *Nadja* (livre de poche), p. 20.

50. *R,* p. 134 (essay on Jules Verne).

51. *Op. cit.* (above, note 43), p. 183.

52. Butor, see Chapter 1, pp. 21–22. Breton, e.g., "Les Mots sans rides"

in *Les Pas perdus* (Editions de la *NRF,* 1924), pp. 167–71: *Point du jour* (Gallimard, 1934), pp. 25–26: "Doesn't the mediocrity of our universe stem essentially from our powers of enunciation? . . . Language can and must be wrested from its state of servitude."

53. Leonard B. Meyer, *Music, the Arts and Ideas* (Chicago University Press, 1967), p. 219.

54. Published together by *Fata Morgana,* Montpellier, 1968, not paginated.

55. The influence of Laforgue is also discernible in occasional lines, and reappears in, e.g., "Hespérides et harengs" in *Travaux d'approche,* Butor's latest collection of poems.

56. *NRF,* XXIX, 173 (May, 1967), 983–96: Albeuve: Castella, 1968 (with "Paysage de Répons"): *Illustrations II,* pp. 40–157, in an entirely different form.

57. Alain Bosquet, "Michel Butor poète," *Le Monde,* June 7, 1969.

58. Chapter 1, p. 20.

59. *Litanie d'eau* (Galerie La Hune, 1964): edition limited to 105 copies. Reprinted, with important variants, in *Illustrations,* pp. 107–87.

60. See Chapter 3, p. 62 and note 30.

61. *Comme Shirley* (Galerie La Hune, 1966): edition limited to 1,000 copies. Reprinted, in an entirely different form, in *Illustrations II,* pp. 38–225 (the original was only 66 lines long). For other examples of humor in Butor's poetry, see the poem on Fourier (above, note 13) and "Blues des projets" in *Travaux d'approche.*

62. See F. Van Rossum-Guyon, *Critique du roman,* pp. 263–77.

63. E.g., p. 375 ("the whole night listening" to "reptiles, the whole night").

Chapter Nine

1. Among the better studies are those by Pierre A.-G. Astier, Ludovic Janvier, John Sturrock, and Gerda Zeltner. See Selected Bibliography.

2. See in this connection an investigation by *Nouvelles littéraires* entitled "Un Peuple de moralistes pourra-t-il accepter le nouveau roman?," and reprinted in R.-M. Albérès, *Métamorphoses du roman* (Albin Michel, 1966), pp. 247–66.

3. *R II,* p. 19 ("Le Roman et la poésie").

4. Sartre in *Les Ecrivains en personne,* p. 216.

Selected Bibliography

(Note: French books are published in Paris, unless otherwise stated.)

PRIMARY SOURCES

Passage de Milan. Editions de Minuit, 1954.

L'Emploi du temps. Editions de Minuit, 1956 (reprinted by Union générale d'éditions, Coll. "10/18," with a postface by Georges Raillard).

La Modification. Editions de Minuit, 1957 (reprinted by Union générale d'éditions, Coll. "10/18," with a postface by Michel Leiris). There are also excellent critical editions by John Sturrock (London: Methuen's Twentieth Century Texts, 1971) and Jacques Guicharnaud (Waltham, Mass.: Ginn and Co., 1970).

Le Génie du lieu. Grasset, 1958.

Répertoire. Editions de Minuit, 1960.

Degrés. Gallimard, 1960.

Histoire extraordinaire, essai sur un rêve de Baudelaire. Gallimard, 1961.

Mobile, étude pour une représentation des Etats-Unis. Gallimard, 1962.

Réseau aérien, texte radiophonique. Gallimard, 1962.

Votre Faust, fantaisie variable genre opéra. Not yet published *in toto,* but extracts published in various journals from 1962 on.

Description de San Marco. Gallimard, 1963.

Répertoire II. Editions de Minuit, 1964.

Illustrations. Gallimard, Coll. "Le Chemin," 1964.

6 810 000 Litres d'eau par seconde, étude stéréophonique. Gallimard, 1965.

Portrait de l'artiste en jeune singe, capriccio. Gallimard, 1967.

Répertoire III. Editions de Minuit, 1968.

Essais sur les Essais. Gallimard, Coll. "Les Essais," 1968.

Illustrations II. Gallimard, Coll. "Le Chemin," 1969.

Les Mots dans la peinture. Geneva: Skira, Coll. "Les Sentiers de la création," 1969.

La Rose des vents, 32 rhumbs pour Charles Fourier. Gallimard, Coll. "Le Chemin," 1970.

Où, le Génie du lieu, 2. Gallimard, 1971.

Dialogue avec 33 variations de Ludwig van Beethoven sur une valse de Diabelli. Gallimard, Coll. "Le Chemin," 1971.

Travaux d'approche. Gallimard, Coll. "Poésie," 1972.

Translations:

Passing Time (*L'Emploi du temps*), trans. Jean Stewart. New York: Simon and Schuster, 1960.

A Change of Heart (*La Modification*), trans. Jean Stewart. New York: Simon and Schuster, 1959.

Degrees (*Degrés*), trans. Richard Howard, New York: Simon and Schuster, 1963.

Niagara: A Stereophonic Novel (*6 810 000 Litres d'eau par seconde*), trans. Elinor S. Miller. New York: Henry Regnery, 1969.

Inventory: Essays, with a foreword by Richard Howard. New York: Simon and Schuster, 1968. Translations by various hands of essays mainly from *Répertoire* and *Répertoire II*.

SECONDARY SOURCES

1. Books:

ALBÉRÈS, R.-M. *Butor*. Editions universitaires, Coll. "Classiques du XXe siècle," 1964. Reasonable introduction to Butor marred by repetitiveness and tendency not to relate theme to form.

ASTIER, PIERRE A.-G. *La Crise du roman français et le nouveau réalisme*. Nouvelles Editions Debresse, 1968. Good account of the "nouveau roman."

BOOK-SENNINGER, CLAUDE and KOLBERT, JACK. *L'Art de Michel Butor*. New York: Oxford University Press, 1970. Useful anthology of Butor's writings with introduction, notes, and vocabulary.

CHARBONNIER, GEORGES. *Entretiens avec Michel Butor*. Gallimard, 1967. Edited transcript of a series of radio interviews, full of interesting comments by Butor on his own work.

ECO, UMBERTO. *L'Œuvre ouverte*. Editions du Seuil, 1965. French translation of work originally published in Italian. Essential for an understanding of the concept of "open-ness."

JANVIER, LUDOVIC. *Une Parole exigeante*. Editions de Minuit, 1964. Difficult but rewarding book on the "nouveau roman."

LALANDE, BERNARD. *Butor: La Modification*. Hatier, Coll. "Profil d'une œuvre," no. 26, 1972. Typically French schematic analysis of Butor's novel.

MERCIER, VIVIAN. *The New Novel, from Queneau to Pinget*. New York: Farrar, Straus and Giroux, 1971. General introduction to the "nouveau roman."

MEYER, LEONARD B. *Music, the Arts and Ideas, Patterns and Predictions in Twentieth Century Culture*. Chicago: Chicago University Press, 1967. Invaluable for "situating" Butor in a very wide context.

RAILLARD, GEORGES. *Michel Butor.* Gallimard, Coll. "La Bibliothèque idéale," 1968. Not for beginners, but well worth the effort of those with a good command of French.

ROUDAUT, JEAN. *Michel Butor ou le livre futur.* Gallimard, Coll. "Le Chemin," 1964. Very perceptive, particularly on thematic aspects of Butor.

ROUDIEZ, LEON. *Michel Butor.* New York: Columbia Essays on Modern Writers, no. 9, 1965. Excellent introduction in English.

STURROCK, JOHN. *The French New Novel.* Oxford: Oxford University Press, 1969. Excellent survey of the "nouveau roman" helped by an awareness of the philosophical background.

VAN ROSSUM-GUYON, FRANÇOISE. *Critique du roman, Essai sur "la Modification" de Michel Butor.* Gallimard, Coll. "Bibliothèque des Idées," 1970. Extremely detailed analysis of Butor's novel based on recent trends in literary scholarship. Probably most useful as a work to be "dipped into."

ZELTNER, GERDA. *La grande Aventure du roman français au XXe siècle.* Gonthier, Coll. "Grand Format Médiations," 1967. Translation of a work which originally appeared in German. Very readable account of the "nouveau roman."

2. Articles and Journals

L'Arc. No. 39 (1969). Number devoted entirely to Butor, including contributions by him.

Les Cahiers du Centre d'Etudes et de Recherches marxistes. No. 62 (1968), "Votre Faust." Contains interviews with Butor and Pousseur, variants, and other interesting items.

Musique en jeu. No. 4 (1971), "Michel Butor et la musique," pp. 63–111. Contains articles by Butor on the influence of music on his work and "Les Mots dans la musique" ("Words in Music"); Henri Pousseur on Butor's *Dialogue avec 33 Variations;* D. and J.-Y Bosseur on *Votre Faust* and *Répons.*

SPENCER, MICHAEL. "*Etat présent* of Butor Studies," *Australian Journal of French Studies,* VIII, 1 (1971), 84–97. Review of about 90 articles, books, interviews concerning Butor.

Index